Astrology

&

Shadow

WORK

About the Author

Catherine Gerdes is an astrologer, writer, and multi-certified coach, accredited by the National Board for Health and Wellness. Her work has been featured in *Well + Good*, *Bustle*, and *Elite Daily*, and she is a featured instructor on Insight Timer. In addition to *Astrology & Shadow Work*, she is the author of *The Little Book of Crystal Healing: A Beginner's Guide to Harnessing the Healing Power of Crystals*. Visit her at Catherine-Gerdes.com.

Astrology & Shadow WORK

Self-Discovery with Your Celestial Compass

Catherine Gerdes

LLEWELLYN
WOODBURY, MINNESOTA

First Edition
First Printing, 2024

Book design by Christine Ha
Cover design by Kevin R. Brown
Interior illustrations
    Astrological and planetary glyphs by the Llewellyn Art Department
    The astrology charts in this book were created using the Kepler Superb
    Astrology Program, with kind permission from Cosmic Patterns Software,
    Inc., the manufacturer of the Kepler program (www.astrosoftware.com,
    kepler@astrosoftware.com).
    Tarot Original 1909 Deck © 2021 with art created by Pamela Colman Smith
    and Arthur Edward Waite. Used with permission of LoScarabeo.

Llewellyn Publications is a registered trademark of Llewellyn Worldwide Ltd.

Library of Congress Cataloging-in-Publication Data (Pending)
ISBN: 978-0-7387-7892-1

Llewellyn Publications
A Division of Llewellyn Worldwide Ltd.
2143 Wooddale Drive
Woodbury, MN 55125-2989
www.llewellyn.com

Printed in the United States of America

Other Books by Catherine Gerdes

The Little Book of Crystal Healing: A Beginner's Guide to Harnessing the Healing Power of Crystals

*For the deep dreamers, modern mystics, and nature seekers
awakening to their cosmic connection.*

☽

Contents

· · · · · · · · · · · · · · · ·

Part Three: Further Exploration

Acknowledgments

To my dear readers, thank you for embarking on your mystically curious quest into astrology. I am grateful for my teachers and mentors in navigating this celestial compass. Thank you to Lia, Nikki, and Rob. Writing is one of my first loves, and this book is birthed, at least in part, as a result of my mom's early encouragement to write and my dad's introduction to archetypes, mythology, and immortal stories. Undeniably, my cherished memories of both nudging my pen to paper contributed to holding this work in my hands. Gratitude and acknowledgment to my grandmother for summoning the courage to share astrological guidance in a challenging era. Thank you to everyone who has a part in distributing, retailing, and sharing this work of mine. Finally, a resounding thank you to the team of alchemists at Llewellyn for making magic with me.

Introduction

As above, so below—what is happening in the cosmos corresponds with the unfolding of events in our lives. There are no coincidences. There are destined moments, and in some cases, there is wiggle room for our free will. But as many of us have witnessed from transits and life events, we don't always have a choice. We might experience a serendipitous meeting or receive a gift or career opportunity. These are like blessings presented to us—and we act on them. Then there could've been times when we were offered an opportunity that we weren't prepared to receive or were shown a new path when we weren't ready to embark on a new journey. There are also major life events, such as natural disasters or diagnoses of loved ones, that we couldn't have done anything to change.

This book is about helping you understand yourself more richly through your chart and teaching you how to make empowered decisions during those windows of time when you *do* have a choice. You are made up of tons of energetic content in the cosmos, and the placements of particular celestial bodies at your time of birth determine your unique composite. Our astrological charts reveal the various aspects of ourselves—our personality, desires, wounds, gifts, and pitfalls—and learning our astrological makeup can fast-track us toward life lessons, reveal relationship patterns, and increase our self-awareness. One of the greatest benefits of learning our charts is that we gain the opportunity to live more in alignment with our authentic wiring through our natal placements, and this allows us to shrug off conditioning that has kept us out of touch with ourselves. This book is meant to inspire, illuminate, and help you discover more of who you are based on your chart's signatures and the gifts divinely planted there. Ultimately, learning your chart enables you to reconnect with yourself. When we lose sight of who we are, our charts have the rare ability to hold up a mirror and remind us. This book will help you use your chart as that mirror.

In addition to being a rich field of study and science, there can also be an intuitive element to our interpretations. As you gain wisdom, I urge you to embrace the foundational knowledge of astrology *and* lean into your intuitive understanding.

Where We're Venturing

While this book will demystify some key elements in your chart, such as the meaning of your moon sign, abundance signatures, and partnership prerequisites, and you will learn to decode some basics of this cosmic language, you can best interpret your natal chart by considering how all parts form the whole. We identify more of our traits by learning about all these components in our charts. But to understand this collective celestial web, we must grasp the basics—and there is a lot we can learn from these separate strands.

First, you'll learn the foundational components, including important terms, the energies of the celestial bodies, and the essentials of your natal chart. Then, through sign-by-sign breakdowns, you'll discover the twelve archetypes of the zodiac. You'll understand your chart's dominant energies through the signs, including your unique associations through colors, herbs, tarot, and more. As we move into more covert realms, you will be given shadow work for addressing blockages and translating cosmic language into self-awareness. Throughout this book, you'll find descriptions that include highlights, or positive magnetic qualities, alongside shadow traits, or challenging facets. Our shadows can include the parts of ourselves we keep hidden or outside our viewfinder, and these can counteract positive developments in our lives. Bringing conscious awareness to these subconscious strands, accepting these parts, or intentionally altering them can bring deep fulfillment and lasting change. While there's no use in vilifying these characteristics that are a part of the full-range spectrum of a sign, the conscious healing of these traits is called *shadow work*. Ultimately, shadow work involves awareness and integration, and it can help you make more empowered decisions. Last, you'll explore themes for growth and empowerment. These include natural blessings and gifts through Jupiter, resilience indicated by Pluto, and how the nodal placements tie into our soul's purpose for a more aligned, fulfilling life.

Each chapter heading provides you with a compass point. For example, if you're curious about the transformative healing traits of Chiron or the sign of Scorpio, you can navigate and learn at your discretion. However, the intention of this book is to provide a rich, holistic awareness of your astrological blueprint. You will learn to bridge the gap between your astrological wiring and practical well-being so that you can heal, transform your life, and thrive.

There's no hierarchy of better or worse personal astrology, meaning no placement or sign is superior. Even the more challenging combinations of energies and harsh aspects provide us with gifts. However, we each have indicators of behaviors that are more accessible and those that can prove more challenging. For example, if you have multiple planets in one sign, that sign's energy can be a theme in your life and easily accessible to you. In contrast, signs with no planets or placements might be more difficult for you to access and understand. Someone with a stellium, or three or more placements together, in Leo could access their creative talents and express their heart-led passions readily. A person with no placements in Aries or the first house may have challenges focusing on their personal life and personal development journey. Our charts clue us in on our natural gifts and which areas of life have hurdles to overcome.

What You'll Need

Before venturing forward, you'll need your chart. You can find yours online at Astro.com, generate it in the Time Passages app, or have one provided to you by an astrologer. You'll need the accurate date, time, and place of your birth. An accurate birth time is valuable since this determines our rising sign, impacting the placements of the planets throughout our houses. While that might not make sense now, it will prove to be important. Also, be sure that Chiron, the asteroid, is visible in your chart. While there are multiple house systems, the one we're working with throughout this book is called Placidus. This is the most common and may be your resource's default setting. But if you're prompted to choose, that is the one you'll want to pick. Once you have your natal chart with this valuable information, you're set.

My Celestial Journey

Astrology was a tool that helped me find nourishment and healing. As I was learning to translate this language of the sky, I gained awareness of the pieces of me I'd overlooked, and I saw where my assets and passions aligned. Preceding my journey of cosmic curiosity, my grandmother was an astrologer—and she hand drew natal charts! I'm in awe of her ability to navigate this information without the support of today's software. She left an incredible gift in the form of three generations' worth of birth dates, times, and coordinates.

While I didn't have the chance to learn from her, astrology felt like a language that had once been native. Investigating my chart and learning the fundamentals required research, but I quickly embraced it, and interpretations clicked. With time and practice, I became a consulting astrologer for publications with upward of fifty million monthly readers, echoing my grandmother's published horoscopes during the "Mad Men" era. I've found satisfaction by reflecting insights to others during one-on-one readings of their cosmic blueprints. Like many astrologers, I imagine that I'll be a student of the stars for life, and I'll continue witnessing glimmers of new insights as various life events unfold.

In addition to better understanding myself through my chart and experiencing multiple *eureka* moments, I started to value divine timing, or the cosmic windows of opportunities provided by the transits. I grew conscious of my connection to a plan and universal energy greater than myself. Seeing this intertwining of our free will and divine destiny was simultaneously humbling and empowering—and this, along with a blossoming of self-mastery, is what I wish for you to find.

But before we begin, here's one pact to consider making with yourself. Since you'll be diving deep into your chart, spare yourself any potential judgment along this journey. In other words, promise yourself that you won't allow a challenging aspect or difficult-seeming placement to get you down. Impactful individuals with incredible life stories have difficult aspects, such as squares and oppositions, in their charts. There are world leaders with challenging Mercury placements (the planet of communication) delivering speeches heard throughout the world. Not only is it possible to turn what you might perceive as self-defeating ick into empowered gold, but placements perceived as challenges in your chart hold the potential to evolve into your super-powers. Before we begin, I suggest making an agreement with yourself. You might call this a spell. Accept that you'll embrace your chart with open arms, and in doing so, allow it to guide you home to yourself. And so it is...

Part One
Laying the Foundation

Chapter One
The Basics

Before we jump into the signs and their shadows, we need to cover some big-picture basics. If you look at your birth chart and think, "I don't know what I'm looking at," don't worry! Throughout part 1, we'll dive into the meanings of your chart's symbols and some foundational terms.

Now that you've downloaded your chart, you'll notice that there is much more going on than familiar sun and moon symbols. Each of us is a complex compilation of many types of energies. Every symbol and its placement offers us clues about who we are. In this chapter, we'll start our learning by zooming out to see the big picture, exploring the elements and modalities. Then we'll cover the twelve houses and main aspects of astrology. Before we dive into the signs, we'll explore the luminaries and planets, including their associations, energies, and how to apply shadow work for each. All this foundational information will enable you to *zoom in* and interpret more specific, unique details within your chart. But for now, the basics.

The Elements

There are four elements in astrology, and each sign embodies one of them. From the densest to lightest, the elements are earth, water, fire, and air. Depending on which element dominates your chart, you can get an idea of how comfortable you are with change and how you relate to others. Understanding the elements will help you see your patterns and embrace your natural talents.

Earth

The earth signs are Taurus, Virgo, and Capricorn. While each earth sign is different, they are all grounded and practical in nature. They are perceived as stable, predictable, and materially focused. Earth energy is tied to money, the physical world, and energy exchanges and is therefore associated with the suit of pentacles in tarot. Of the tarot's four suits—pentacles, swords, cups, and wands—the pentacles are the most tangible and impenetrable item. The nature of the pentacles mirrors the steadiness and reliability of earth signs. Earth signs benefit from opening to shifts in their routine and trying new things, and this can be embodied through aiming high into an airer realm. They can utilize air's lighter density to open to different perspectives. Diving into the unseen through spiritual practices can balance their natural focus on the concrete world. Those with less earth energy in their charts benefit from incorporating intentionality, grounding, and stability into their daily life.

Water

Cancer, Scorpio, and Pisces are the water signs. Water signs are emotionally connected, intuitive, and sensitive. They are represented by the cups in the tarot, which are tied to relationships and feelings. Water signs have the ability to feel through the emotional pendulum,

from deep grief to great love. Their wiring may lend them clairsen-
tience, or sudden insight into the emotions of those around them.
With these gifts of sensitivity and relatability, inner check-ins around
their own needs are essential. Their energy is a resource, and it must
be managed appropriately for their well-being. While submersion
into emotional depths can be a potent asset, it doesn't benefit them or
their loved ones for them to stay there. They benefit from transmuting those deep feelings into practical action (incorporating the elements of earth and fire) or direct communication (the element of air).
Those with less water in their charts can find this emotional range
difficult to navigate and can benefit from diving into their creative
outlets or performing intentional grief work.

Fire

The fire signs are Aries, Leo, and Sagittarius. Fire signs are passionate and the most action oriented. They can naturally enliven a space
or conversation. Signified by the wands in the tarot, the fire element
is tied to manifestation, boldness, and movement. When aligned with
their purpose, fire signs naturally act toward their desires. Their association with boldness thrusts them into new situations, and of
the four elements, they can be most susceptible to outsourcing their
sense of self-value to the impressions of others. It's crucial that they
self-validate without seeking external confirmation of their greatness
and worthiness. Also, taking action has its benefits, but not if it's bypassing what's going on beneath the surface. Fire signs should be wary
of repressing emotions and benefit from intentionally channeling
their pent-up emotions into their work. Those with less fire in their
charts may need a little extra *oomph* to get plans off the ground and
make moves—especially as it relates to changing their circumstances.

Air

Gemini, Libra, and Aquarius form the air sign trio. Air signs are the most cerebrally connected and can resort to head-over-heart decision-making. As the least dense element, air signs are swift. Their high vantage point gives them perspective, and they can offer others a sense of understanding and problem-solving. They see through a different lens, but the distance that this vantage point requires can make them seem aloof or detached. The energy of air is connected to communication through messages, connection through thoughts, and comfort found in intellectual pursuits. Simply, air signs are associated with the mind, truth, and intuitive messages. While air signs must embrace their rational and analytical minds, they must also recognize how comfortable they are spending time in their heads and avoid overthinking. Thought loops don't serve them, and dwelling is unlikely to determine outcomes. Air signs benefit from surrendering to the present moment and abandoning their worries of the past and future. Those with less air in their charts can benefit from intentionally mapping out various competing perspectives and expanding their outlooks beyond their comfort zone.

Applying the Elements

As you learn your chart, pay attention to which signs and their elements have placements. (Placements are indicated by the icons sprinkled throughout your chart, and for our uses in this book, the term *placements* includes the planets, the asteroid Chiron, and other points, including the ascendant and the nodes, which we will discover in later chapters). Notice how many placements you have in fire signs, water signs, etc. Which signs and elements appear to have no placements? You might find that you have planets equally spread across the different elements in your chart, but one element is often underrepresented in a chart. If this is the case, you might find yourself craving the energy of that element or sign. For example, if you have little water energy in your chart, or minimal placements in water energy, you may crave being near water and benefit from doing intentional emotional, therapeutic work instead of thinking about or suppressing your feelings.

Now, notice the dominant elements that show up in your chart. These are the signs where you have many placements, and the themes of these elements are easily at your disposal. For example, if you have lots of placements in air signs, your life themes will revolve around mental strategy, communication, and imagination. These themes will come naturally to you, as you are simply utilizing your dominant elements in your everyday life. Therefore, you will witness those as personal strengths and may benefit from intentionally incorporating any underrepresented elements.

The Modalities

There are three modalities, or qualities, for each of the signs: cardinal, fixed, and mutable. Like the elements, the modalities reveal how we feel most comfortable navigating our lives and relationships, and they show us our relationships with the turning over of life's seasons. Cardinal energy offers initiative, fixed energy is stagnant or reliable, and mutable energy gives us the capacity to shift and adapt. We need each of these to take meaningful action in our lives. There are four signs associated with each of these energies, and each of these modalities has light and shadow traits.

Cardinal Energy

The cardinal signs are Aries, Cancer, Libra, and Capricorn. Cardinal energy's motto is "Let's get it started." They are comfortable making decisions and taking action and can be well connected to their drive. This ability to initiate is a gift and shouldn't be taken lightly. Since their decisions impact others, they must exercise discernment and avoid impulsivity. When too spontaneous, the consequences can be damaging, which is part of their learning in this lifetime. Conversely, they are not fixed energy; they are not *meant* to remain stagnant or allow others to dictate plans. Balanced, mature cardinal energy will selectively initiate and move with considerate intentionality. This ability contributes to their leadership skills, and others can look to them to navigate groups. In addition to using thoughtful judgment, cardinal signs benefit from collaborating and understanding the vantage points of others.

If you have a lot of cardinal energy, you are meant to initiate projects, start trends, and get things off the ground. You might not be the person following through on the project, and that's okay. It's important to consider what is needed and lacking in the world and listen to your inner wisdom for what you want to create. For guidance, notice what naturally excites you and where you're stirred to contribute. You are not meant to follow the crowd; you are meant to lead them.

Fixed Energy

The fixed signs are Taurus, Leo, Scorpio, and Aquarius. Fixed energy's motto is "Steady as she goes." They are inclined to make stable decisions and play it safe. They take the baton from cardinal energy and move with consistency and persistence along the path in front of them. Their strength in staying the course can become incredible manifesting energy, as their gradual effort can result in rewards. However, they can be rigidly averse to change and benefit from incorporating flexibility into their plans. This inherent strength of dependability can result in the digging in of heels if they aren't careful.

For their growth, those with strong fixed energies benefit from inner check-ins around their rigidity. Consistency comes naturally, so monitoring this and surrendering rigidity will enhance their relationships. The fixed signs are learning the art of surrendering to the Universe and divine timing. They are learning the lessons of opening to transformation as well as the benefits of cutting their losses. Most of all, they are detaching their sense of self-value from perceived loss and inevitable change.

If you have a lot of fixed energy, you are here to provide foundations and stability. This gives grounding and predictability to your partners, colleagues, environment, and yourself. Since both cardinal and mutable energies involve movement, you are here to counterbalance those energies and remain on course and, when it's appropriate, embrace surrender.

Mutable Energy

Gemini, Virgo, Sagittarius, and Pisces make up the mutable signs. Mutable energy's motto is "Let it flow." Mutable signs are the most flexible to change. This is reflected through the seasons, as every equinox occurs at the culmination of mutable seasons transitioning into the start of cardinal seasons. As the equinox marks summer's transition into fall, mutable Virgo season culminates, and we shift into the cardinal season of Libra. As the most adaptable modality, mutable signs are riding the wave of unpredictability and adventure. In relationships, they bring natural flexibility to the table. They must be careful, as this adaptability may make them susceptible to overwhelm or overriding their plans for others' needs, leaving them feeling resentful and disconnected from themselves. To address this shadow of self-abandonment, they must be aware of their natural flexibility and identify moment-to-moment whether their actions are aligned with their needs. They should avoid domineering relationships and benefit from incorporating focus and grounding into their plans. They benefit from recognizing the gift of their flexibility and directing their intention into projects aligned with their desires and relationships aligned with their values.

If you have a lot of mutable energy, you are meant to shift, and this causes changes in relationships and your environments. You can activate a new path for others or offer a fresh perspective, and your malleability can help transmute existing systems through periods of evolution. You are capable of inner transformation, too, and at times will need to incorporate stability and grounding into your routine. You are a changemaker, and instigating cultural or personal shifts may happen in unconventional ways.

The Overarching Energies

The four elements and three modalities are basic but necessary, allowing you to understand the qualities of signs before you learn them individually. Let's tack on the houses to provide meaning to the visible framework of your natal chart.

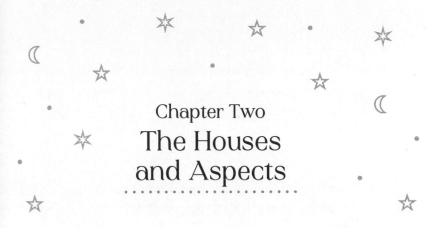

Chapter Two
The Houses and Aspects

Like pieces of a pie, our charts are divided into twelve sections, referred to as the houses. The houses are a helpful framework for beginning to navigate your chart. Looking at the sample chart, we can see that the numbers for each house are located around the innermost circle. You'll notice these start with the first house on the left and move sequentially counterclockwise around the chart. In this example, Libra is the sign of the first house and the individual's rising sign. This means that Libra's diplomatic, indecisive, and Venusian traits are associated with this person's relationship with themselves (first house themes) and how they interact with the world (rising sign). Despite their sun in Capricorn, which denotes structure, reliability, and ambition, they are viewed as a Libra with Venusian traits and interpret the world through this lens.

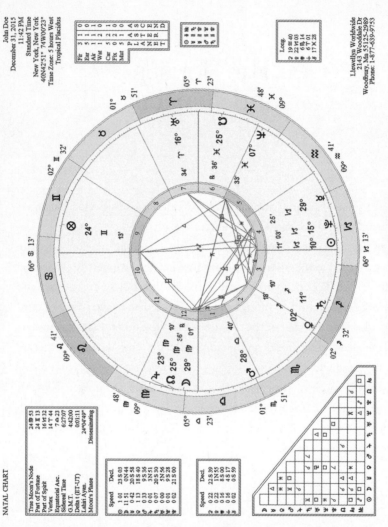

Sample Astrological Chart

Each house is associated with different themes, and the signs associated with each house in our charts lend greater insight into how we approach the house's themes.

If you have one or many placements in one house, the themes of this house are focal points for you. It's the combination of house, planet, and sign that weaves a greater story. For example, your sun in Virgo in the fifth house indicates that you connect with yourself and feel energized through creativity and possibly healing, research, medicine, or storytelling. Maintaining your routine and incorporating daily rituals are essential. Expression is a key part of your life's journey, and connecting with your inner child is important for you. However, observing this placement in its shadow, you hold a high standard in your creative life, and perfectionistic tendencies can stifle your free, creative expression. Knowing when to lower the bar for your work will be crucial, and accepting imperfection in yourself will be essential for progress.

The First House

The first house is associated with the self and physical body. Outside of the first house, we begin dealing with things, people, and concepts outside of ourselves—but the first house is intentionally self-focused. It can reveal aspects of our appearance and our sense of identity. Since the sign of our first house is our ascendant, this sign reveals how we interact with the world and how others perceive us. The best way to work with the first house is through gaining self-knowledge or personal development work. The shadowy trap of first-house energy can be self-absorption or disconnection from our sense of self. This can happen when there are challenging or multiple energies in the first house, which we'll cover later in this chapter. Each house has a sign associated with it, even if these don't correspond with your chart. So, while your first house is most likely *not* Aries, this house is associated with the sign of Aries because it is the first sign of the zodiac. For example, my first house is Gemini. This reveals that communication and writing are integral to my sense of self and impact how others perceive me. Curiosity and flexibility are important for navigating my life and learning more about the world.

The Second House

This house's themes include finances, assets, personal values, and self-worth. This house clues us in on information regarding our personal possessions but not our combined assets with others. In addition to resources, it reveals our relationship with our energy and time. The best expression of second-house energy is resource management and self-love. The shadow of the second house is greed, low self-worth, and poor management of time and resources. This house is connected to the sign of Taurus.

The Third House

This house is connected to themes of communication, mental processing, and local community. Here we can learn about our immediate surroundings, such as our neighborhood, as well as our siblings. The third house shows us how we process information and connect with others. Positive third-house energy manifests as harmony in our community and skills in our communication. Challenging energy in the third house can cause miscommunication, disturbances in our community, or disconnection with siblings. Examples of challenging energies here include feeling restricted in communication with the confining nature of a Saturn placement or fiery, aggressive communication with Mars. These placements in the third house can also represent more difficult times in our elementary school years. The positive expressions of third-house energy are connection and curiosity, and the shadows are overthinking and gossip. Gemini is the sign associated with the third house.

The Fourth House

This house carries the themes of family and home. This house can show us our private life and relationship with our abode and indicate what makes us feel secure. Harmonious fourth-house energy indicates stability in our home and private lives. Difficult energy here signifies disruption in familial relationships or personal affairs. In its positive expression, the fourth house reveals stability; in its shadow, it reveals insecurity. For example, Pluto in the fourth house can reveal disruption and control issues within family, and Venus in the fourth house can indicate pleasant energy and enjoyable dynamics at home. This house is tied to the sign of Cancer.

The Fifth House

This house's themes are children, pleasure, dating, and creativity. This is one of the houses that reveals artistic abilities and can show how we have fun. Self-expression, romance, and relationships with children, as well as with our inner child, are found here. The best manifestation of the fifth house indicates ease in self-expression, powerful creativity, and pleasurable friendships and dating lives, which could be revealed through Jupiter or Venus in this house. Difficult fifth-house energy, such as the presence of Pluto or Saturn, signifies strained relationships or disconnection from our joy, pleasure, or creativity. The most positive embodiment of the fifth house is healthy self-expression, and its shadow trait is vanity or muted expressiveness. This house is connected to the sign of Leo.

The Sixth House

This house has themes of health, work, and daily routines. Information in this house can reveal our work ethic, relationships with co-workers, and potential health issues. This is also the house associated with pets. Positive expressions of sixth-house energy include comfort with routines, harmony in the workplace, and ease in resolving health issues. Difficult sixth-house energy manifests as issues in the workplace, struggles with routines, and potential wellness woes. A Scorpio sixth house can reveal tricky and transformative health situations, and a Libra sixth house can reveal pleasant but self-sacrificial relationships with colleagues. Working with the sixth house in a beneficial way can involve taking care of our health and maintaining structure in our lives. The shadow of the sixth house is taking health for granted or being too rigid with our routine. This house is associated with the sign of Virgo.

The Seventh House

This house's themes are partnerships and marriage. This house is where we find relationships that are typically nonfamilial by birth and can reveal marriage contracts, business agreements, and close relationships. A constructive embodiment can indicate pleasant relationships or marriage, which can show up through Jupiter or Venus in the seventh house. A challenging expression of the seventh house signifies struggles in relationships, including romantic or business partnerships. This challenging expression could be shown through Pluto or Mars placements in the seventh house. The positive side of the seventh house involves interpersonal harmony, and its shadow involves disagreement, people-pleasing, or lack of compromise. This house is tied to Libra.

The Eighth House

This house holds the themes of shared resources, sex, and spirituality. This house can reveal information related to debts, taxes, inheritances, secrets, and our relationship with mysticism. Positive energy in the eighth house, like Jupiter, can signify the understanding of hidden knowledge, including spiritual and intuitive connectedness. This can also indicate success and financial gains from working with others. Trying eighth-house energy points toward debts, challenging entanglements, or transformative experiences. These challenges could arise from Pluto or Saturn placements. Positive use of eighth-house energy is vulnerability and reciprocity, and the shadows are inauthenticity, withholding information, and obsession in partnerships. This house is connected to the sign of Scorpio.

The Ninth House

This house has themes of higher learning, religion, philosophies, and beliefs. This house reveals information regarding long-distance travel and publishing as well as information about gurus, teachers, or professors. Pleasant ninth-house energy can indicate finding meaningful mentors and educational opportunities or the ability to become an impactful teacher or guide. Some ways this could manifest are through a Leo-ruled ninth house or from Jupiter placed here. Challenging ninth-house energy signals difficulty with higher systems of learning, hurtful or ineffective mentors, and strains in teaching others. Having Aries ruling the ninth house or Pluto in the ninth house could connect to these challenging experiences. Positive ninth-house energy manifests as the exploration of ideas and faraway places, and the shadow is in the know-it-all. This house is connected to the sign of Sagittarius.

The Tenth House

This house has themes of career and reputation, and it indicates information related to our legacy. The tenth house opposes the fourth house of our private lives and represents our public life. Public status and recognition are revealed here. Positive tenth-house energy, such as sun or Venus placements or a Leo-ruled tenth house, could manifest as success in a career, high achievements, and a glowing reputation. Challenging tenth-house energy can indicate struggles in a long-term career, a damaged reputation, or a tumultuous public life. This challenging energy could be connected to Chiron placed here. The shadow-to-light spectrum to explore within the tenth house is the robotic corporate climb versus the purpose-driven career. This house is tied to the sign of Capricorn.

The Eleventh House

This house encompasses friendships, technology, and long-term gains. This house shows our connections with like-minded people, including acquaintances. It can reveal unconventional thoughts or innovative aspirations and is the house of astrology. Elevated expressions of eleventh-house energies include meaningful friendships, long-distance connections, and opportunities through technology. These expressions might happen from Venus here or Libra ruling the eleventh house. Difficult eleventh-house energy can manifest as travel complications, friendship difficulties, or technical issues. This could be expressed through Uranus or Neptune here or through an Aries eleventh house. The light-to-shadow spectrum for the eleventh house is connection over ideas versus subscribing to groupthink. This house is tied to the sign of Aquarius.

The Twelfth House

This house holds the themes of spirituality, dreams, and the astral realm. Along with the fourth house, information in this house can be tied to our ancestry, and as with the sixth house, it is associated with service. The twelfth house is also tied to addictions, self-sacrifice, mental health, and hidden enemies. Significant twelfth-house energy may indicate repeated needs to surrender. Beneficial expressions of twelfth-house energy might be spiritual enlightenment, dream awareness, astral connectivity, and healing community. This could be tied to Jupiter or the sun here. More difficult expressions of twelfth-house energy can be rumination, isolation, and struggles with mental health. This could express through having Chiron or Pluto placed here. The light-to-shadow spectrum to explore with the twelfth house is solitude and renewal versus isolation and escapism. This house is connected to the sign of Pisces.

Houses in Your Chart

The houses reveal the sections of our lives that will require greater focus. Through planets, luminaries, and asteroids sprinkled throughout, the houses paint a picture. Note which houses you have lots of placements or activity within. Investigate the themes of these houses and which events have transpired in these facets of your life. For the most part, an empty house indicates that the house's themes may not be major focal points in your life. The themes of an empty house might be more like supporting roles, whereas houses with placements, especially many planets or a stellium, are the leading players in this lifetime. If you'd like more clarity on your empty houses, look to the house's ruler. For example, if an Aries eleventh house is empty, look where its ruler, Mars, and its aspects are. In this example, wherever

Mars is in this person's chart can provide clues around the eleventh house themes of friendships and technology.

Here's another general way of looking at the houses. While others can play minor characters, houses one through six are personal houses. These reveal the continually developing relationship we have with ourselves. While houses seven through ten also involve ourselves, they are more interpersonal areas of our lives. Houses eleven and twelve really illuminate the bigger picture through a combination of philanthropy, humanitarianism, service, and even martyrdom. Some charts will express lopsided energy, revealing focal points that are personal, interpersonal, or big picture in scope. Of course, there's no right or wrong distribution of celestial bodies throughout the houses. But this assessment can lend guidance around which areas of life require more energy and provide deep lessons. Now that you've toured through the twelve houses, let's dive into the communication channels between the planets, luminaries, and asteroids: the aspects.

The Aspects

Aspects are the ways the celestial bodies "speak" with one another. These are the relationships formed between the planets, asteroids, and luminaries in our charts. These are represented by all the lines moving through the middle of your chart and are determined by the separation of specific degrees between the celestial bodies. Each aspect reveals the harmony, synergy, or tension formed between different energies, and these are messages revealing which parts of our lives might prove more challenging or feel more carefree. That difficult chemistry is referred to as harsh aspects, and some of these are *squares* and *oppositions*. But this tension offers the opportunity to overcome challenges, and approaching these through a lens of overcoming is the best way to work with harsh aspects. The easygoing chemistry is found within the soft aspects, such as *sextiles* and *trines*. These have harmonious energies and indicate ease and flow in certain parts of our lives. Technically, *conjunctions* are harsh aspects, but sometimes we can utilize these as strengths.

Prior to learning these five major aspects, start with grasping the foundations we've covered. In fact, these aspects might be the last part of your foundational learning, which has included the elements, modalities, and houses. Beginning with the basics will prevent you from feeling overwhelmed or misinterpreting aspects in your chart, and once you have grasped the planets in each of the signs and houses, you can begin to interpret the aspects formed. This will allow you to combine these compartmentalized pieces into a larger story. Also, the degrees allowed for each *orb*, or correlation formed between close degrees, slightly vary by astrological school of thought. But the closer the degrees within the orb, such as zero, one, or two degrees, the more exact the aspect and the more impactful the message. Harsh aspects reveal areas of life that challenge one another, and keeping this in mind can help us navigate scenarios more intentionally. For example, with placements in the fourth house of family square placements in the seventh house of marriage, conflicts can be expected, but at times interactions can be intentionally dodged, or you can prepare to navigate disagreements. Overall, when applying shadow work to the aspects, the goal is to attempt to harmonize the difficult aspects and embrace the harmonious ones.

Conjunction

Points in exact conjunction are at a zero-degree angle from one another, resulting in the closest aspects formed. Conjunctions are formed within a zero-to-ten-degree orb. Placements in conjunction with one another intensify each other's energy. Depending on the involved planetary energies, these can be challenging or harmonious. Any placements in a conjunction represent the energies that will consistently impact one another in your life. When interpreting these placements, remember that they aren't meant to be separated. Since these are based on degrees, they can still form a conjunction, even in separate houses or signs. As an example, Mars conjunct Mercury could manifest as a quick-thinking, fast-talking individual who drives like a racer on their morning commute. Jupiter conjunct Venus could emphasize pleasure, romance, and beauty in one's life, but this pair conjunct can also represent high spending. Understanding these tendencies embedded in either example can be helpful to these natal placements for utilizing or tempering these energies.

Stellium

While a stellium is technically not an aspect, when three or more planets are conjunct, or tight together like peas in a pod, they form a stellium. This is a concentration of planets or asteroids. A stellium's presence in your chart indicates an important signature, and the closer the degrees within this orb, the more potent the energy. This sign and house will be significant in your life, and its themes can pull your focus and energy toward them. For example, a stellium formed in the sign of Gemini could suggest an emphasis on broadcasting or writing or on life themes of curiosity and community, and a stellium in the fifth house could indicate life themes involving creativity, expression, and children or childlike qualities. Unlike the aspects, a stellium isn't signified through a symbol in our chart.

Sextile

The sextile is found within a sixty-degree angle. Sextiles are formed within a zero-to-six-degree orb. A sextile is a harmonious aspect of energies that are supportive of one another. Each sign has two opportunities for sextiles, found two signs away in either direction. For example, if Jupiter sextiles Venus in your chart, this could suggest ease with moneymaking or abundant opportunities for love and dating. Themes of money, beauty, or charm could be accentuated. As another example, if Uranus forms a sextile with the moon, there is a relationship between one's emotions and potential volatility. To work with this placement, this person would want to be intentional with healing and honor feelings as they surface.

Trine

This aspect is found within a 120-degree angle. Trines are formed within a zero-to-eight-degree orb. A trine is a strong, positive aspect forming this bond between two energies. Trines tend to be tied to luck and are formed between placements within the same element. So, as a sign, Taurus trines both Virgo and Capricorn. As an example using planets, Mercury trine Neptune emphasizes dreamy and creative communication that can be tied to one's spiritual life. Pluto trine the sun could give an empowered boost to personal expression and confidence, but it could require tempering of control within one's environment or criticism around oneself.

Square

As the name suggests, this aspect forms a ninety-degree angle. Squares are formed within a zero-to-eight-degree orb. As one of the most challenging aspects, a square indicates conflict, energies that do not see eye to eye and stifle the needs of the other. These occur between signs with the same modality (Aries squares Capricorn and Cancer). For example, moon square Mercury presents challenges with understanding and communicating feelings. These two energies, involving emotions and sharing, are at odds and can cause struggles for this individual. Relationships can require deliberate effort to clearly express and process emotions with others.

Opposition

This aspect is formed by a 180-degree angle. Oppositions are formed within a zero-to-eight-degree orb. As another challenging aspect, an opposition suggests tension between two or more energies. Imagine each energy pulling their agenda in the opposite direction from the other. You might think of this as a power struggle. For example, the moon opposing Neptune could lead to a chasm between fantasy and reality at times. On the other hand, with this placement, someone could feel too grounded, practical, and cut off from their creative abilities, including the ability to dream and fantasize. Another example would be Saturn opposing one's ascendant. This could create tension as controlling partners could attempt to control this person's expression or the way they interact with the world. In this instance, domineering relationships could become problematic, and this person would benefit from addressing this or avoiding these dynamics.

The Framework Is Built

The houses cover every facet of our personal and interconnected lives. Understanding the aspects positions you to see how the celestial bodies communicate with each other and impact real-world events in your life. You are learning the alphabet of astrology. Once you understand the planets and signs, you'll form words and be able to string together sentences or interpretations based on these communication channels of aspects and particular house themes. Let's explore the planets.

Chapter Three
The Luminaries and the Planets

. . . .

Each of the planets holds a unique energy that is predictable in nature and a specific window of time in which they transit through the signs. The inner planets, or planets closest to the sun, include Mercury, Venus, Earth, and Mars. The outer planets, or those farthest from the sun, include Jupiter, Saturn, Uranus, Neptune, and Pluto. Aside from the planets, we have the luminaries: the sun and the moon.

The transits of the inner planets impact us on a personal level and are more specific to our individual charts. The outer planets are specific to entire generations, and since their transits impact large groups, they can mark world events and cultural trends. During each planet's retrograde, or reverse course through a sign, the time it spends in an individual sign lengthens. Sometimes people fear having retrograde planets in their chart—but this is not a marker of doomed destiny. Retrograde planets in the chart could denote a need to be patient around that planet's energy or signify that its lessons or gifts come later in life. It might require self-reflective work to identify how to better work with the planet's energy, or there could be a block to remove in accessing it. Often, these retrograde placements are signified through a red font or designated with an *R*. Also, particular signs cater nicely to a planet's energy, while others simply don't mesh well together. The terms denoting this are *exalted*, *detriment*, and *fall position*. When a planet is exalted, its qualities are supported, and this energy can shine. When a planet is in its detriment, it is positioned across from and in opposition to the sign in which it rules. This stifles its energy and can make its potency harder to access. And when a planet is in its fall position, its energy is in a weak expression. This position is in direct opposition to its exaltation position.

Planets can also be in their *domicile* position. A planet's domicile is its home position or the signs it rules. This powerful placement can emphasize a planet's energy in your chart and life. So, for each sign association listed, this is also where the planet or luminary is in its domicile.

Before you begin applying this information to your chart, I suggest just noticing where these fall on the zodiac wheel. This will help lay a foundation for learning. Then, look at your own chart and, as we move through each planet or luminary, notice which ones might be in any positions of exaltation, detriment, fall, or domicile.

The Sun and the Self

Sign Association: Leo
House Association: 5th
Transits Each Sign: Every Thirty Days
Themes: Self, Expression, Ego, Personality, Father
In Detriment: Aquarius
Exalted: Aries

In Fall: Libra
In a Quote: *"Not I, not any one else can travel that road for you.*
You must travel it for yourself." —**Walt Whitman**

The sun is a giver of energy and life, and it draws energy toward it. Our sun sign defines us, revealing our personality traits and characteristics of our nature. As a radiant celestial body, this is where you shine and, through embodiment, how you are more likely to find success. Our sun sign isn't some fixed fate as much as it is an archetype we are learning to embody; this is who we are continually becoming. With the planets revolving around it, the sun represents our ego. Our sun sign can also reveal characteristics about our fathers—or a strong paternal energy in our lives. While the sun rules the fire sign of Leo, it is exalted in the fellow fire sign Aries, and as the luminary associated with the self, it connects with Aries's association with the personal first house. The sun, connected to self or soul, doesn't shine so brightly in Libra, the sign of partnership. This is the sun's fall or weak position.

The Sun and the Ego

Our sun placement is tied to our ego and, on a deeper level, to our soul's expression. Ego has been given a bad rap, but it's certainly not all bad. In fact, it can be necessary. Just as the signs and planets exist on a spectrum, this luminary and the ego also contain a range. Understanding this range helps us express our sun placement and connect with ourselves.

When we lack a healthy sense of self-worth, we must cultivate self-love or a healthy boost to our sense of self. This lack of self-connection is one polarity found within this spectrum. When over-inflated, the ego moves to the opposite end of the spectrum. It's arrogant and self-important without the capacity to connect to or appreciate the light within others. No matter the sign, the sun's ideal expression is not devoid of radiance on one end or in a battle to out-shine on the other extreme. It's not desperate for applause, but it isn't self-deprecating. It glows, beams, and shines its light.

Shadow Work: The Sun and You

As you learn your sun sign, explore how your sun sign's traits might repress or overexpress and how this has manifested in your personal expression and connection to yourself. Look to the celebratory traits of this part of the zodiac. Your essence radiates through these quali-ties. Likewise, open to the shadow work portion of this sign. This can illuminate the ways you may block your light from radiating. Look to the associations with your sun sign and see how each of these reso-nates in your personal life. As an example, if your sun sign is Aquarius associated with the eleventh house of networks and friendships, re-flect on how these relationships have helped illuminate parts of your-self, how these relationships have inspired you, and how you've made an impact in these circles, too.

The Moon and Our Feelings

Sign Association: Cancer

House Association: 4th

Transits Each Sign: Every 2.3 Days

Themes: Feelings, Mood, Home, Intuition, Mother

In Detriment: Capricorn

Exalted: Taurus

In Fall: Scorpio

In a Quote: *"The feeling is often the deeper truth, the opinion the more superficial one."* —**Augustus William Hare**

Our moon sign clues us in on our emotional landscape. Although not a planet, the moon carries a gravitational pull, and its phases mirror the waves of our emotions. Or, since the moon is the luminary associated with feelings, you might say that our emotions are being pulled and impacted by its phases. The moon reveals the shifting moods through each sign's expression as it moves quickly through the zodiac.

Our individual moon sign reveals how we process and express our feelings. It reveals how we find security and nurturing. When we feel overwhelmed or encounter a trauma, our moon placement can show how we self-medicate or encourage ourselves. Our emotional triggers can be revealed through the shadow traits of our moon signs. Understanding the moon signs of our loved ones can clue us in on how we can comfort them in the most impactful way. Our moon sign can also reveal attributes of our mothers, or a maternal figure in our lives. The sensitive moon is exalted in Venus-ruled Taurus, finding comfort and strength in this feminine, sensory sign. Scorpio's fixed water, or ice, is harsh and intense for the moon.

Moon and Our Sense of Home

Our moon placement reveals a story, but the element attributed to the sign of our moon placement can lend information about what type of place we might feel most comfortable living and establishing our home in. If your moon placement is in a fire sign, you might thrive in a warmer climate. You could crave a place filled with action—whether that action is external and buzzy or internal, inspiring you to move your body. If your moon is in an earth sign, practically understanding your emotions and feeling supported by your environment are essential. At home, feeling cozy on the couch, having plentiful food options, and feeling nurtured by practical things will be impactful and pacifying.

If your moon is in an air sign, your feelings may shift or drive you to act impulsively. In home decisions, you need to feel a sense of freedom, even when planting solid roots. You might feel comfortable living abroad or taking a sabbatical. For moon placements in water signs, there can be an intuitive element to your domestic decisions, including scouting out a location that connects with your inner knowing and decorating in a way that creates the right vibe. When you don't feel well or connected to your sense of self, you could be inspired to clean your home, decorate with natural elements, and incorporate the water element into your abode through fountains, fish, or flowers to bring fresh energy into your space.

Moon Stages and Our Routine

One complete moon cycle consists of four main moon stages, and each stage transmits a different influence. These four cycles are the new moon, waxing moon, full moon, and waning moon.

The new moon signifies the dawn of something new and can mark a new chapter in our lives. You may wish to start a new personal venture, promote a new service, or present something new about yourself at the time of a new moon. The slate is clean, and the opportunity is ripe.

On the waxing moon stage, the energy is building. This is a great time for preparation and planning. You might benefit from working in a meditative flow state receptive to twists and turns as they arise. You might want to be in creative vision-building mode to take full advantage of this energy.

On the full moon, the energy has culminated to its fullest point. This is a time for release and surrender. When launching during the new moon and creating during the waxing moon, you may arrive at some conclusions about what you must surrender for yourself or your process to move forward. The full moon gives you the opportunity to use that awareness and surrender what isn't working. Sometimes, you might find that there's nothing for you to do. In that case, you'll want to allow whatever isn't aligning to release itself as you move ahead on your path.

On the waning moon, the energy is dissipating. This is the opposite of that slow and steady build we feel during the waxing moon. This is the preparatory stage for the new moon, where we wipe the slate so we can build anew. Now is a time for cleansing our space or relinquishing a bad habit that might have sprung into our awareness around the full moon.

In addition to the four main moon stages, we experience eclipses. Eclipses are significant, ushering in a time of fated or destined change. Eclipse cycles occur twice per year, and they contain two eclipses within the same lunar cycle, or month. During the eclipse cycle, a solar eclipse occurs at the new moon phase and a lunar eclipse occurs on the full moon. There is nothing to do during these cycles but surrender to any changes showing up for us. The best way to work with this energy is not to overcommit. Take it easy, and instead of attempting to force a desired outcome, allow change to transpire.

Shadow Work: The Moon and You

Reflect on how the attributes of your moon sign mirror your relationship with your emotions. Look to the unique traits of your moon sign, and open to the shadow work portion found in that sign's chapter. This section can reveal the ways you may struggle with metabolizing challenging feelings. Overall, it should reflect information about how you experience relationships and process emotions. Some gifts can be found here, too. As an example, if your moon sign is Virgo, you might impose high standards on yourself and overanalyze your feelings, and you may resonate with having healing capabilities and guiding others through grief.

Mercury and Our Mindset

Sign Association: Gemini and Virgo

House Association: 3rd and 6th

Transits Each Sign: Approximately One Month

Themes: Mind, Communication, Intellect, Changeability, Manifestation

In Detriment: Sagittarius

Exalted: Virgo

In Fall: Pisces

In a Quote: *"Don't wait for the stars to align, reach up and rearrange them the way you want… create your own constellation."* —**Pharrell Williams**

There is a correlation between the energy of the planets and multiple mythological gods, including those of Greek and Roman mythology. Hermes in Greek mythology, and Mercury in Roman myths, was the mythological messenger known for communicating among the gods and being the cleverest among them. He served as a protector for travelers and the god of sleep and dreams.

As the fastest planet in the solar system, our Mercury sign and house reveal how we communicate and process information. Because of its association with swiftness, our Mercury placement can signify which area of life we crave information about and where we grow restless. Mercurial energy can show us where we are gifted, original, and able to create. There can be an intuitive element to this area of our lives. The element of your Mercury sign is revealing, as well. For example, Mercury in earth signs can be methodical, careful, and reserved in their communication. Communication may be more emotional, sentimental, and vulnerable in a water sign. A fire sign Mercury placement can be dramatic or theatrical in their communication. They can also quickly come to conclusions, and their movements can be erratic in response to fiery thoughts. Mercury is propelled in an air sign, and they can be fast talkers, devour content, and swiftly change their minds. Mercury finds strength in Virgo's analytical home, where it is exalted. Mercury doesn't understand the dissolving of boundaries inherent to Pisces, and this combination can require greater intentionality to discover clarity.

Shadow Work: Mercury and You

Look to the sign and house where you have Mercury and the themes associated with this placement. This is an area of life where, like Mercurial energy, you might move fast and communicate well. This can also be an area of life where you consume content and crave understanding. As Mercury is tied to the energy of manifestation, it can also be a part of your life where you feel natural inspiration. Reaping the rewards from this part of your life could require clear intention, thought, and interaction.

Mercury Retrograde

Each of the planets goes through retrograde, or reverse course, phases. The length of time varies depending on the planet. When a planet goes retrograde, we can experience blockages around the themes of that planet. Sometimes, an old issue or situation resurfaces, and we can choose to behave differently or face the fated lesson associated with that situation. The often talked about retrograde phase is Mercury retrograde, and this transit generally takes place three times per year.

During a Mercury retrograde, communication can be challenging. You can find yourself more tongue-tied or managing technological issues. Digital work might require more time and patience, or you might postpone a project. During this transit, travel delays can be more common. Mercury retrogrades teach us to be patient and remind us to surrender. Whatever *it* is for us, *it* doesn't always arrive according to our timing. It's from these perceived glitches that we can find gratitude for seasons of smooth sailing.

Venus: Love and Money

Sign Association: Taurus and Libra

House Association: 2nd and 7th

Transits Each Sign: Approximately One Month

Themes: Love, Money, Sensuality, Charm, Beauty

In Detriment: Aries and Scorpio

Exalted: Pisces

In Fall: Virgo

In a Quote: *"Style is the answer to everything. A fresh way to approach a dull or dangerous thing. To do a dull thing in style is preferable to doing a dangerous thing without it. To do a dangerous thing with style is what I call art.... Boxing can be an art. Not many have style. Not many can keep style.... Style is the difference, a way of doing, a way of being done."* —**Charles Bukowski**

Associated with Aphrodite in Greek mythology and Venus in Roman mythology, Venus represents love, beauty, pleasure, sex, and fertility. As its symbol suggests, it is associated with feminine energy. Our Venus placement teaches us about our financial habits as well as how we express love and how we desire to receive it. It can reveal our values, what we honor within ourselves, and how we demonstrate self-love.

Venusian energy connects us with our senses and pleasure, and the sensation of a bubble bath, the taste of biscotti, and the smell after the rain are all within the realm of Venus. While enjoyable, these are fleeting pleasures. As the quote for this sign suggests, the shadow side of Venusian energy involves superficiality.

Our Venus placement clues us in to our sense of style, relationship with aesthetics, and home and décor preferences. In relationships, Venus manifests as superficial charm, short-term flings, or misjudging long-lasting potential in someone only to discover a lack of staying power. When it comes to lasting partnership and marriage, this is the realm of Jupiter. But Venus can reveal our love language and information relating to children in our charts—or qualities we embodied in our younger years. Venus is exalted in romantic, dreamy Pisces, where this softness is well suited. Opposing Pisces, Venus falls in the analytical, critical sign of Virgo.

Venus is the ruler of Taurus and Libra, and you might notice these Venusian themes are highly prioritized by your Taurus and Libra friends—even if this is just their sun sign. In your connections with them, you may witness how they derive gratification from life's simple pleasures and remain fulfilled by their connection to their senses.

Venus transits each sign for about one month, so it is never far from our sun sign. While Venus is in retrograde, it is advised not to change your physical appearance. This can be a time of regretful decisions surrounding beauty or love, and it's best to wait and reconsider changes once Venus is moving direct again.

Shadow Work: Venus and You

Look to the sign and house where Venus sits in your chart. Notice which themes of that sign and house resonate with you, and consider the connection between these themes and your sense of pleasure, values, and joy. Contemplate how this house and sign inform your personal ways of relating to others, including what you enjoy receiving from others and how you express love to them. Explore how this sign and house are related to your relationship with money and resources. Looking to the house themes, is this an area of life that has required a lot of your investment—both resources and energy? You are likely to notice a connection between your child and your Venus sign, too. If you have children, explore the relationship between your child's personality and the attributes of your Venus sign.

Mars and Our Drive

Sign Association: Aries and Scorpio
House Association: 1st and 8th
Transits Each Sign: Approximately Two Months
Themes: Action, Sex, Passion, Drive, War
In Detriment: Taurus and Libra
Exalted: Capricorn
In Fall: Cancer
In a Quote: *"The question isn't who is going to let me; it's who is going to stop me."* —**Ayn Rand**

As its symbol suggests, Mars is tied to masculine energy. Mars is the god of war in Roman mythology and is associated with Ares in Greek mythology. This association with war reveals Mars's traits and the potential for battle and ambition in our charts. Mars energy is fiery, passionate, and action oriented. It can embody aggression or drive. While Mars was acknowledged for courage in Roman history, taking on a noble and admirable role, in Greek history, Ares was viewed as ruthless.

As the ruler of the first cardinal sign, Mars is about learning how to take the lead. At its least conscious representation, this means our delivery might be rash, and our actions could prove impulsive. At its most conscious, Mars energy has a sense of direction and moves confidently forward. Our Mars placement reveals where we'll assertively invest our energy, what we defend, and the attributes of our sex drive. As a sign of achievement and ambition, Mars is exalted in Capricorn. It *understands* how to utilize courage and intention to complete tasks. Opposite its exaltation position, Mars is at its fall position in Cancer. The watery tides of emotional (and sometimes impulsive) Cancer can be a precarious placement for Mars, weakening its strength.

The house where Mars resides in our charts reveals our tendency to move quickly and where we push naturally. The element of our Mars sign reveals our motivation or strategy for movement, such as heightened practicality in earth signs, emotional movement in water signs, natural passion in fire signs, or mental strategy in air signs.

Shadow Work: Mars and You

Look to the sign and house where you have Mars and the associated themes. This is an area of life where, like Martian energy, events can move swiftly, and you might be more impulsive. It can reveal where you could encounter abrasive energy or where you might need to embody your inner warrior. It can also suggest the area of life in which you invest your time and focus—consciously or unconsciously. Look to the themes of this house to see which area of life you exert great willpower in. Look to the characteristics of this sign to add more depth to your sense of drive and commitment.

4

Jupiter and Our Luck

Sign Association: Sagittarius and Pisces

House Association: 9th and 12th

Transits Each Sign: Approximately One Year

Themes: Luck, Expansion, Growth, Opportunity, Life Partner

In Detriment: Gemini and Virgo

Exalted: Cancer

In Fall: Capricorn

In a Quote: *"Everything I touch is a success."* **—Louise Hay**

Jupiter in Roman myths is associated with Zeus in Greek mythology, and he was responsible for overseeing all aspects of life and coined the god of thunder. In Roman mythology, he wielded many powers and was closely associated with fate and the capability of changing life events.

In our charts, Jupiter is the great benefic, or bestower of blessings. Abundance and opportunity are indicated through our Jupiter placement, and it benefits us to approach this part of our lives with an optimistic attitude. Here, we see how we might receive blessings or the associations where we receive fortunate opportunities and luck. This placement can also lend information regarding long-distance travel and feelings of expansiveness. It can uncover which field of study or area of life captivates us and where we can experience great opportunities and accolades. But Jupiter doesn't do all the heavy lifting. We must apply effort—there might be an element of taking a risk to unlock this placement's inherent rewards. Jupiter also represents a spouse or the qualities we seek in a long-term romantic partner.

Jupiter is exalted, or in a position of strength, in Cancer. The water element combines well with the abundance of Jupiter. Across the axis in Capricorn, Jupiter is in its fall position or a place of weakness. Cardinal earth imposes uncomfortable rigidity on Jupiter's expansive nature, which thrives in movable terrain.

Shadow Work: Jupiter and You

Look to the sign and house where you have Jupiter and the themes associated with these. This is an area of life where, like Jupiterian energy, we may be blessed or stumble across opportunities just for us. This can be an area of life where you're perceived as lucky or feel fortunate. The themes of your Jupiter placement's house can be easy to grasp. They can reveal your personal gifts, and investing energy into fields associated with this sign or house can be beneficial for you. It may also lead to financial gain. Investigate how flexibility could benefit you in this area. Is this a place where you feel the cup is half-full? This is also connected to partnership. Look to the sign's qualities of your Jupiter placement for insight into traits you admire in romantic partners and those which are compatible with you for long-term love.

Saturn and Responsibility

Sign Association: Capricorn and Aquarius

House Association: 10th and 11th

Transits Each Sign: Approximately 2.5 years

Themes: Restriction, Discipline, Justice, Time, Father

In Detriment: Cancer and Leo

Exalted: Libra

In Fall: Aries
In a Quote: *"Discipline is the bridge between goals and accomplishment."*
   —Jim Rohn

Saturn in Roman myths is associated with Cronus in Greek mythology, and he was the god of agriculture. The energy of Saturn is connected to wealth, time, and maturity, and it is tied to themes of personal harvest and cosmic justice. If the land is acknowledged and tended to, you will reap the benefits (i.e., you reap what you sow).

As our disciplinarian, Saturn doesn't let us bypass life's lessons, as these become our soul's lessons. Saturnian energy wants us to grow, and its method for development is restriction, discipline, and hard-earned rewards through work. Saturn also rules time, and just as the greatest payouts can come over a stretch of time with consistent effort applied, Saturnian lessons require patience and work to reap the benefits. Just as Jupiter wants to bestow blessings but must be met with small effort, Saturn molds us into maturity through deep commitment to tasks—and there are no shortcuts. The themes associated with the house of our Saturn sign can reveal where we should adopt the motto "slow and steady wins the race." This placement can be our key teacher of discipline, and implementing patience benefits this part of our lives. With Libra's association with scales and justice, Saturn's adherence to structure and integrity makes Libra a natural place of exultation, or strength. But across the axis in the impulsive cardinal fire sign of Aries, Saturn's restrictive nature is weakened, or in its fall position.

Saturnian energy is paternal in nature, and how our Saturn placement aspects our sun sign or moon sign can reveal characteristics of our relationship with our fathers or paternal figures.

Shadow Work: Saturn and You

Look to the house and sign that you have Saturn in and the associated themes to reveal which part of your life requires consistent focus and hard work. These placements can also reveal which part of your life you benefit from taking your time to assess and where you can grow if you devote intentional energy. For example, Saturn in the second house will reward you for structure and dedication to your finances. Creating order by sticking to budgets is one way to work with this placement. Since the second house is also tied to self-worth, creating a long-term plan and continually raising the bar around income as you invest in your skill sets will pay off. With time and intentional focus, your personal assets can grow.

No matter the personal Saturn placement, we might feel like the bar is set higher for us in this area of our lives. Our Saturn placement can reveal where we will learn challenging lessons and, as a result, where we can build resilience. As a planet associated with time, the themes of this house will require patience. There can be a theme of rewards with Saturn, and there is a correlation between our devotion and investment with tangible benefits blossoming in our lives.

Saturn Returns and Personal Growth

Specific transits indicate life-changing chapters in our lives. One of these is our Saturn return, when Saturn returns to its original placement in our natal chart. Our first Saturn return happens around the age of thirty.

This serves a great purpose as our cosmic coming-of-age. No matter the legal age of maturity or cultural benchmarks that recognize us as adults, our Saturn return is when we're tasked with taking responsibility. If we've been attached to a victim story or undervaluing ourselves, this two-plus-year cycle pushes us to reclaim our energy. For some, this might feel like a crisis, or a relationship might end. This is one of the greatest transits for eradicating lack mindsets and pushing us toward greater personal sovereignty and self-trust. At this time, challenging life lessons provide the opportunity to metabolize old wounds that have separated us from recognizing ourselves as treasures.

Sometimes, we have the choice of learning the lesson or sliding through the cracks of it. If you successfully bypass what you perceive as disaster and uphold the status quo, you'll never know what gifts would've awaited you on the other side of your surrender. A future transit, possibly involving Saturn, could come along with the same message, and once there's more at stake. Do you notice how sometimes the same lessons show up in different people? Surrender is the name of the game with this Saturnian energy, and just as the stern parent has good intentions, these Saturnian transits are moving us toward our destiny. As much as Saturn returns get doused with shade, they are opportunities to move through portals into new relationships with ourselves.

Also, Saturn transiting our eighth or twelfth houses—both houses of spirituality—can present challenges or personal growth opportunities. Saturn through the eighth house brings lessons around energy exchange and shared resources. Saturn in the twelfth house can bring existential questions related to our connection to the Universe, the afterlife, or the astral realm. This twelfth-house transit can also involve deep dives into our subconscious or ancestry.

Uranus and Our Rebellious Streak

Sign Association: Aquarius

House Association: 11th

Transits Each Sign: Seven Years

Themes: Unconventionality, Change, Erraticism, Progress, Originality

In Detriment: Leo

Exalted: Scorpio

In Fall: Taurus

In a Quote: *"The only way to deal with an unfree world is to become so absolutely free that your very existence is an act of rebellion."*
—**Albert Camus**

Uranus (or Ouranos) in Greek myths is associated with Caelus in Roman mythology, and this deity was the literal sky—in a similar way that Gaia was the earth. Uranus held powerful psychic capabilities and is associated with astral travel. He is sometimes connected to Heaven.

As the planet of revolution and innovation, this isn't the energy of the wallflower. The energy of Uranus is finding freedom and genuine expression. Our Uranus placement indicates an area of our lives where we might be seen as unconventional and trailblazing. This is where we seek freedom. Our Uranus house placement is where we revolutionize, buck trends, and stand apart from the status quo—where we will need to chart our own course. Since Uranian energy involves shock and erraticism, this can also be an area of our lives where we experience unexpected or traumatic events. Despite the planets holding predictable energy, Uranus can be predictably unpredictable. Uranus is also associated with brisk travel, erratic communication, and spirituality. Uranus is in its fall position, or weakened, in Taurus, where consistency reigns and the erraticism that Uranus can bring is not welcomed. Since Uranus is one of the generational planets, it reveals a theme of a generation and where its members feel an innate responsibility to break free.

Shadow Work: Uranus and You

Look to the house and sign where you have Uranus and the themes associated with these. This placement can reveal where we disturb the status quo. We might be trailblazers or revolutionaries in this area of our lives. As you buck trends in this part of your life, you might be viewed as an outcast or feel like one. It can also be where you find spiritual connection and are ahead of your time. In this house's themes, you can see where you can face surprising events or shocking reveals. For example, if Uranus is in your seventh house, your approach to business partnerships and marriage will rebel against the status quo. You can also encounter surprises in your partnerships. This placement requires us to think on our feet, and similar to Saturn, it reveals tests that can strengthen our resilience in this compartment of our lives.

Uranus Opposition and Soul Development

In addition to a Saturn return, we might deeply evaluate our lives from a bird's-eye view just after the age of forty. This perspective flip and life revaluation coincides with our Uranus opposition. This transit occurs around the age of forty-two, when transiting Uranus opposes our natal placement of Uranus. During this transit, we can initiate breakups or sudden life changes. The theme of freedom becomes significant, and where we don't feel free is on the chopping block. The devotion of our energy and resources might come into question for a reassessment and, ultimately, for shifting more into alignment with our true values. If our current career or relationship isn't aligned with those values, we'll likely venture on to a new course. If we haven't already, we may start questioning our legacy and what we're leaving behind.

Neptune and Mysticism

Sign Association: Pisces
House Association: 12th
Transits Each Sign: Approximately Fourteen Years
Themes: Dreams, Mysticism, Delusion, Dependence, Creativity
In Detriment: Virgo
Exalted: Leo
In Fall: Capricorn
In a Quote: *"My story isn't pleasant, it's not sweet and harmonious like the invented stories; it tastes of folly and bewilderment, of madness and dream, like the life of all people who no longer want to lie to themselves."* —**Hermann Hesse**

Neptune in Roman myths is associated with Poseidon in Greek mythology. Neptune is the god of the sea and is connected with wind, storms, and water. Often seen with a trident, he is emotionally volatile and instigates storms and earthquakes.

Neptune is one of the planets tied to spirituality, and it's linked to our dream space, the astral realm, and our creativity. It can show us where we have intuitive insights or receive spiritual information.

It can also reveal the part of our lives where we experience a disso-lution of boundaries or where we might flow instead of forcing our more concrete goals or desires. This can be where we creatively in-dulge, can be prone to obsession, and wear rose-colored glasses that skew our reality. At worst, this can be where we lie to ourselves—and the personal growth for this placement comes from seeing things for what they are, not what we'd like them to be.

The house themes of our Neptune natal placement might benefit from more practicality and realism. We should understand that there is fog here and that we will benefit from defining our standards or creating boundaries. Like Uranus, Neptune is a generational planet, and it reveals the collective area that a generation views through this dreamy lens. Dreamy, creative Neptune is in its fall, or weak position, in Capricorn. Capricorn is the sign of achievement and corporations, and the CEO doesn't don rose-colored glasses.

Shadow Work: Neptune and You

Look to the sign and house where you have Neptune and the associ-ated themes. Themes of creativity, spirituality, and an overall dream-iness can be interwoven into this house's themes. Since Neptune be-stows rose-colored glasses, exercising some caution is advised here. We tend to romanticize this pocket of our lives, and this placement can indicate where we'll benefit from gaining awareness of misunder-standings or seeing illusions in others. As a planet tied to addiction, this is a place where we benefit from exercising self-awareness. From time to time, this is where you might notice a trend of choosing op-timism over practicality and where an inquisitive nature will benefit you more than taking things at face value. For example, with Neptune in the sixth house of work and routine, your imagination or brain-storming could play a part in your professional life. There might be haziness in your perception of your coworkers. Creativity is likely to play a role in your daily habits and routine. Since this is a house of health, you'll want to be cautious around your relationship with any substances, food, or beverages that could negatively impact your well-being.

Pluto and Our Transformation

Sign Association: Scorpio
House Association: 8th
Transits Each Sign: Eleven to Thirty Years
Themes: Transformation, Destruction, Excavation, Death, Rebirth
In Detriment: Taurus
Exalted: Aries
In Fall: Leo
In a Quote: *"I'm interested in that thing that happens where there's a breaking point for some people and not for others. You go through such hardship, things that are almost impossibly difficult, and there's no sign that it's going to get any better, and that's the point when people quit. But some don't."* —**Robert Redford**

Pluto in Roman myths is associated with Hades in Greek mythology. He was the god of the underworld and tied to the afterlife. Pluto translates to the "wealthy one," so he can also be associated with affluence. With its existential themes, this is the realm of deep transformation.

A dwarf planet, Pluto is connected to the Scorpionic topics of transformation, sex, and death. It is an intense energy, probing beneath the surface of the themes associated with the house of our Pluto placement. As the planet of death and rebirth, this part of our lives is connected to our personal power and can indicate where we seek control or where others seek it over us. This part of our lives generates controversy and a hurdle to overcome, and it is commonly related to trauma. Ultimately, this indicates the area in our lives where we can undergo transformation for the sake of empowerment.

For half of the year, Pluto is in retrograde motion. There's a vast gap between the number of years it takes for slow-moving Pluto to transit through each sign, and depending on which one, this span of time ranges from nearly eleven to thirty years. Pluto moves on an elliptical orbit and bolts swiftly through Scorpio (the sign it rules) while trickling through Taurus (the sign of its detriment). A generational planet, Pluto's movement through a sign reveals its themes being unearthed, examined, and transformed. With its lengthy journey, Pluto shows an area in which a generation is transforming as well as their relationship to power surrounding the themes of this sign. For example, the Pluto in Scorpio generation is transforming themes involving sex and gender identity awareness and highlighting a resurgence in the mainstream popularity of astrology and tarot. Pluto in Libra generation, or Gen X, represented the offspring following the normalization of divorce. Their themes for transformation have involved paving a new way forward for marriage and relationships—including the normalization of midlife partnerships.

Future generations can benefit as each Pluto generation transmutes energy and transforms these themes. Look to your Pluto placement and the theme of this sign to see its impact on the collective change taking place. You've witnessed these themes in your own life and in the lives of your peers. In the sign of Leo, Pluto is in its fall, or weakened, position. Pluto's underworld does not fare well for the radiance of the sign ruled by the sun. Because of its association with destruction, Pluto energy poses a threat to self-expression here.

Shadow Work: Pluto and You

Look to the sign and house where you have Pluto and the associated themes. These themes are a deeply transformative part of your life's journey. This is an area of life where you hold personal power but where you can experience tension and power struggles with others. Tied to control, consider how this theme has appeared in the area of your life associated with this house's themes. As a planet of secrets and psychology, how has hidden information played a role in this area of your life? Despite Pluto's shadows, this is a house placement where you can witness empowerment. This might be a house where your gifts shine or where you can transform yourself or others. For example, Pluto in the ninth house can reveal great potential in guiding and teaching others, and taking a leadership position could be a powerful, impactful role to embody. Instead of allowing the tension of transformative Pluto to shrink you, allow the lessons of this sign and house to embolden you. Don't shy away. Lean into it.

Chapter Four
The Signs and Shadow Work

The first thing most of us learn about astrology is our sun sign; some attach their cosmic self-awareness to this and stop here. But, to greater or lesser degrees, we carry components of all the signs, and each one influences some part of our lives.

The twelve signs are broken down by about thirty days. Since we are this composite of varying amounts of these twelve, we understand some of these archetypes over others. The signs that dominate our charts give us more psychological material about who we are, including what drives us and how we express ourselves. We may misunderstand those with the sun signs we lack placements in within our charts. As a simple example, if you don't have placements in Virgo, you might not appreciate the analytical nature of a Virgo sun and misunderstand their constructive criticism. But when it comes to the elements, those that are lacking in our charts indicate the energy we seek to incorporate into our lives. For example, if you lack water sign energy and have lots of fire sign placements, you might feel a stronger pull toward bodies of water or a desire to live seaside.

The signs are not one-dimensional expressions that we are doomed to become. They are multidimensional, complex archetypes with a range of tendencies and traits. The spectrum of characteristics each of them exemplifies includes unique, celebratory qualities as well as shadowy attributes with potential pitfalls. For example, Virgo carries crippling criticism but also impressive self-mastery. Pisces can embody creative ingenuity or tortured artistry. Aquarius is either tied to the community in ways that drown out its unique voice or is the idiosyncratic leader of the group. Throughout this spectrum, there are behaviors and characteristics that we societally judge as *good* or *bad*, and these *bad* traits can be referred to as our shadow traits.

Understanding the shadows involved with our signs—sun, moon, and rising—and doing inner work, or shadow work, can launch us into our next chapter. Shadow work means examining our traits or behaviors that don't serve us well, embracing the pieces in need of healing, and making courageous shifts in response. This involves a subconscious deep dive into parts of ourselves we were taught to keep hidden, parts that we may be terrified to excavate, examine, and heal. Moving through shadow work requires relinquishing control over an aspect of our lives, often something from the past and something we've attached to our sense of self or ego. When we take the time to do shadow work, the goal is to get to the root and heal the damage left unaddressed. When we address the shadows, we can feel freer and more easily navigate through life. This is called integrating our shadow, and all practical application of astrology for our inner work is addressing our shadow and embodying the gifts in our charts. Part of what makes astrology incredible is its mirroring ability to reveal our blind spots.

Investigating the multifaceted nature of the dominant signs in our charts is the beginning step in embodying the pieces of these archetypes already within us—while consciously shrugging off the aspects we wish to release. We can make a conscious choice to release these lower vibrational expressions of the signs. We aren't beholden to becoming a version of our astrological charts that we don't wish to express or be—and shadow work can help us get closer to our most authentic expression of self.

The Tarot and the Signs

The tarot is an ancient divination tool spanning multiple continents and centuries and encompassing a range of archetypes or stages within life's journey. It tells a story through archetypes and symbolism and can help us develop a deeper relationship with our intuition. Each sign is connected to the meanings of the tarot, and each sign is represented by one main card within a group of cards referred to as the major arcana. A sign's major arcana card reveals more personality traits through its imagery. In sequential order, the major arcana cards of the tarot take us along the hero or heroine's journey as embodied by a character referred to as "the Fool." In this way, the tarot, like the signs, reveals the next step in our evolution.

While many renditions of decks have been produced, any specific features in these descriptions are based upon the traditional Rider-Waite-Smith deck. Each card holds one meaning in its upright position and a related but different one in its reversed state. Generally, the reversal of a card can be viewed as its shadow side. When learning the upright and reversal positions explained for your sun, moon, and rising signs, consider how you've embodied these archetypal energies at points along your journey. If you choose to explore the tarot deck for yourself, you may find that specific details make their way to the main stage for you to notice. Consider looking into the symbolism that draws your eye or piques your curiosity. There can be a pertinent message to discover. Likewise, as you read through the meanings of these specific cards connected to your signs, you may feel captivated by an element or theme, even without the deck. That can hold something to explore along your personal shadow work voyage. The tarot is an excellent tool to practice shadow work, and understanding the meaning of these specific cards and the signs they represent contributes to this.

Critical Degrees

In addition to their modality, element, and tarot card, the signs have multiple associations, including a color, ruling planet, motto, and more. Each sign holds degrees from zero to twenty-nine. But each degree is associated with a specific sign, which lends further material to our interpretations of each placement. While these degrees hold wisdom worthy of a separate deep dive, there are two particular degrees to highlight. Take a moment to check for zero or twenty-nine degrees in your chart. As the furthest extremes within each sign, these are critical degrees, and they hold special meanings. These can be particularly potent and sensitive. If you witness a zero-degree placement in your chart, picture this as the early stages of learning this placement's energy within this sign and house. When it comes to interpreting this placement, you are in the infancy stages of exploring this lesson. The embodiment of the zero degree can be a bit volatile. For example, a Leo sun at zero degrees can either show up glowing, radiant, and prepared for showcasing creativity, or they could fall subject to self-criticism or doubt. In this instance, they might not seem or feel like a Leo. But there's an innocence to a zero-degree placement that can allow for open-mindedness, opportunity, and exploration, and in this sun sign example, it's in relation with oneself. If you have a twenty-nine-degree placement, the cycle and learning associated with this placement are culminating. Sometimes, this is referred to as the anaretic degree. You might envision this as a graduation from this life lesson. For example, Pluto at this final degree in the fifth house of romance could be relinquishing controlling dynamics in dating and finding empowerment through creative projects, personal expression, and pleasure. Outside of these two, the degrees and any of the sign associations are material to note. But don't let yourself get overwhelmed by them.

Interpreting Our Sun, Moon, and Rising Signs

Some of our most important placements are our "top three," or our sun, moon, and rising placements. We can learn plenty of information from these placements; with these interpretations, we evolve out of the simplistic trend of sun-sign astrology. When we think of ourselves, we might combine the themes of our sun (personality), our rising (how we experience and exchange energy with our environment), and our moon (the way we experience or process our feelings). However, the truth can be more nuanced. We might show up in the world as a bright, sparkly Leo sun or rising, but our capacity to dive into the depths and sit with grief could be exemplified through a Scorpio moon. Your sun, moon, or rising might be in harsh aspect to each other, such as your sun squaring your moon or sun opposing your rising sign. In these instances, we benefit from returning to our awareness of ourselves. It can be necessary to express feelings more readily or act in alignment with what makes us truly happy, especially when our top three are in harsh aspect to one another.

In other cases, you might have your rising and moon in the same sign or your sun and rising together, forming a conjunction. This allows you to clearly express feelings (with the moon) or personality (with the sun) and carries the message for the world that "what you see is what you get." When conjunctions are formed in any of our top three, less is hidden. In my chart, my sun and rising are conjunct in Gemini. I consider this to be beneficial for others and myself—what you see are Gemini traits, and these are true to my sense of self and expression. But my moon is square these placements. Intentionally sharing feelings is an important life theme. My rising sign squaring off my moon means that while suppression is sometimes easier, it's important to give my feelings attention and expression—even when it's not what others anticipate.

The sign at the start of our first house shows us our ascendant, or rising sign, which is indicated by an *AC*. This will always be the "starting line" of our first house. Looking at your chart and returning

to the sample chart on page 18, notice that more than one sign can oc-
cupy the entirety of each house. In the sample chart, Libra is the first
house, even though the early part of Scorpio is within this house, too.
In this example, Libra is the rising sign.

In the sample chart, Venus, Libra's ruling planet, is the chart ruler.
This person may emphasize the senses in daily life, valuing life's little
joys and weaving them into daily rituals. They may have a heightened
or important relationship with food, scents, or luxury. In your chart,
look to the planet ruling your ascendant sign. Since this is your chart
ruler, it is an important energy to grow familiar with and observe. In
your natal chart, the aspects it forms with other planets and luminaries can carry significant messages. When this planet retrogrades, you
might feel these effects more than most retrogrades, and you may feel
an energetic slowing down, experience déjà vu moments, or review or
reflect on something from your past.

While our sun sign reflects our personality and our moon sign reveals
our emotional landscape, our rising sign reveals how we interact with
the world and digest information. Characteristics of our rising sign and
its house uncover the way others perceive us or how we show up in the
world. This is what people notice about us. Sometimes, this is referred to
as the "mask we wear," even when we aren't aware of this impression.

Along with our Venus placement, our rising sign can indicate physical features or our style. Notice the element of your rising sign. This element will be the language that resonates most with us and how we learn
and interact with our surroundings—whether through the mental understanding of air, experiencing through feelings of water, the direct par-
ticipation of fire, or tangible transactions with the earth element.

Like your ascendant sign, you have a descendant placement, often
indicated by DC, directly opposing your ascendant in your seventh
house. This placement can give us clues about our past lives, hint at

ways of being that come naturally to us, and indicate the qualities we seek in a life partner.

Understanding Your Chart

As you continue, read the signs of your sun, rising, moon, and Venus placements. Also, see which signs have lots of activity in your personal chart. You might be an Aquarius sun with intense Scorpio energy, showing up through a stellium in Scorpio. If this is the case, you might hear, "You don't seem like an Aquarius," and you probably don't identify as much with the unconventional, detached energy of Aquarius—or the air element in general. You may be more mysterious and secretive and enjoy researching spirituality, psychology, or more intense topics. If you see lots of activity in a sign, read about this sign and reflect on those attributes within yourself. For any sign that has a stellium, the shadow work for this sign could be particularly useful for you.

Also, notice the signs associated with each of your houses, as this reveals further information. For example, if Sagittarius is the sign ruler of the seventh house of partnerships, this indicates that you value learning through knowledgeable partners, crave a sense of freedom within commitments, and are attracted to fiery and exciting qualities in companions. Or, if Scorpio is the ruler of your tenth house, you may find themes of transformation relevant to your career and reputation. With this placement, your intuition and feelings could be necessary for success, and your focus on career and public life could be obsessive. Once you grasp the knowledge of the signs, you'll string it together with your awareness of the houses and form more fluent conclusions from your chart. Let's look at a celebrity example.

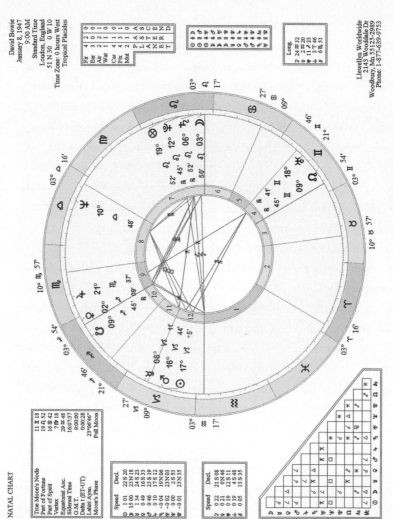

Sample Astrological Chart of David Bowie

In David Bowie's chart, Aquarius is his rising sign and the sign ruler of his first house. This reveals his idiosyncratic, nonconforming image and signals that others could view him as futuristic and otherworldly. We witnessed this throughout his well-documented career, seeing him expressing himself as Ziggy Stardust or performing his song "Life on Mars." His Sagittarius tenth house of career reveals that he was adventurous, bold, and knowledgeable in his field. If he ever struggled in his career, leaning into Sagittarian attributes and furthering his skill sets would've been a way to work with his chart. Professionally, like the bold archetype of the archer, he took risks that were met with the abundance and luck of Sagittarius's ruling planet, Jupiter. His Gemini fifth house of creativity signifies that language and being a wordsmith were important components of his expression and artistry.

In the following chapters, we'll explore the nooks and crannies of each of the twelve signs. From Aries to Pisces, you'll understand the personality of each sign. Since each of these lies within your unique chart, you can benefit from reading each sign for its specific house— regardless of planetary placements in each. Or you may rush toward better understanding your sun, moon, rising, and Venus placements. Either way, you'll have the opportunity to explore the practical ways these twelve energies manifest, including their shadow sides, and become equipped with practices tailored to each one.

Part Two
Understanding the Signs

Chapter Five
Aries

Υ

Theme: The Brave Trek
Archetype: The Warrior
Dates: March 21–April 19
Motto: "I am."
Ruling Planet: Mars
House: 1st
Degrees: 1, 13, 25
Modality: Cardinal
Element: Fire
Color: Red
Body Correlation: The Physical Head and Brain
Keywords: Daring, Impulsive, Independent, Enthusiastic, Initiating
Tarot Card: The Emperor

Characters and Celebrities with Aries Energy
+ Ares
+ Marcus Aurelius

* Alexander the Great
* Genghis Khan
* The Flash (DC Comics)
* Lady Gaga

Aries Playlist

* "Wanna Be Startin' Somethin'" by Michael Jackson
* "Love Is a Battlefield" by Pat Benatar
* "Don't Stop Me Now" by Queen
* "Make the Road by Walking" by Menahan Street Band
* "Never Too Much" by Luther Vandross
* "i" by Kendrick Lamar

Herbs and Supplements for Aries

* Turmeric for anti-inflammation
* Yarrow for overheating
* Maca for adrenal support

Crystals for Aries

* Carnelian for connecting with inner drive
* Red jasper for grounding
* Celestite for peace

In a Quote

"Sometimes your only available transportation is a leap of faith."
—**Margaret Shepard**

As a cardinal fire sign, Aries is the initial spark that sets off a bonfire. As the first sign of the zodiac, they are learning life through firsthand experiences and eagerly rolling up their sleeves for life's tasks. They embody taking the leap, initiating the task, and charting the course. The first four signs—Aries, Taurus, Gemini, and Cancer—are in the process of learning their elements. Since fire is volatile, the channeling of that inner spark makes all the difference in the life of an Aries. Embodying a lit match, Aries must be self-directed and not carelessly thrown. Their inherent comfort with risk can be to their detriment, and learning to cool off their fire and use it constructively can be a lifelong journey.

Each sign is signified by one specific symbol. For Aries, it is the ram, symbolizing their ability to plow ahead. The headbutting ram contains the energy of their ruling planet, Mars. At its best, Mars showcases drive and the will to boldly act. In its most destructive manifestation, Mars is war. Aries, when your fire is not channeled, how do you maintain the peace? Is it worth maintaining? And as the initiator of the zodiac, you may begin to wonder: Must I always lead the charge?

In the Tarot

The Emperor is the tarot card for Aries. Sitting on his throne, he embodies authority, stability, and strength. He is an obvious leader and has significant responsibility. He has fought many battles and successfully climbed the ranks to get to his position. The Emperor is a well-respected and courageous figure. Mature and conscious, the Emperor is one of the embodiments of the divine masculine energy in the tarot deck.

THE EMPEROR.

Aries Sun

An Aries sun is *the* trailblazer. This person dances to the beat of their own drum, and once they have their vision set, they'll move swiftly in its direction. They infuse their actions with passion and their big "why," and there is a short tether between their feelings and their willingness to act. Just as they move swiftly, they tend to think and speak quickly, too—and their words are driven by their emotions. They can be naturally ambitious and goal oriented. They don't always make hasty decisions, but they are capable of reckless choices. They benefit from finding calm, grounding, and presence in the moment. They are more suited to leadership than following others or taking orders and can find satisfaction in guiding groups. They are one of the few signs with an inherent optimism. They take risks, revel in their victories, and experience life in passionate and interactive ways.

Aries Rising

An Aries rising experiences life head-on and through physically engaging with the world. Exercise can provide a panacea for their stress or the natural heat they accumulate within. They can be a bit of a fire starter, and similar to Aries sun, they are quick to act, speak, or send messages. Generally, they don't shy away from confrontation and exert more effort in conversations and relationships than others. When attempting to make their point, they can be perceived as aggressive. While others may find them intimidating, this perceived aggression doesn't always reflect how they feel. If they find an investment worth their energy, Aries rising will give 100 percent of their effort. But over time, this initial devotion can lead to burnout or lack of follow-through, extinguishing the flames of their intention. Aries rising benefits from considering that their self-assertion has the capacity to block their desires. They should avoid combativeness. Asking themselves, "Is this the war I'm willing to wage?" or "Is this a battle worth fighting?" will help them avoid draining their energy through unnecessary spats.

Aries Moon

An Aries moon tends to be independent, driven, and courageous. As the first sign of the zodiac and holding cardinal energy, they can have impulsive tendencies tied to their feelings. Despite being a fire placement, an Aries moon can be emotional, accessing the full gamut of their feelings. They can be bold and brash with the capacity to inspire others. They can nurture themselves by avoiding impulsivity or repressing emotions, and they must channel anger in a productive way.

Aries moons benefit from engaging in self-soothing activities and healthy communication and being in cooling, serene environments. To relax, they can incorporate the element of water into their lives, taking soothing baths or resting near water. When it comes to creative work, they benefit from experimentation. They need to feel free from confinement and allow their creativity to shine. As cardinal fire, if something isn't working, they can and should start over without clinging to a past creation too tightly.

Venus in Aries

In a phrase, this is a "keep it hot!" placement. Venus in Aries is passionate and loves to try a new hobby or activity. It comes naturally for them to take initiative in matters of love, money, and their values. They can appreciate public displays of love and get bored easily. They tend to be flirtatious and, for better or worse, love a good chase. They like to move quickly in life and relationships, and although they must be cautious of being hot-tempered or competitive, they can forgive and move forward. They should avoid impulsive spending. In moneymaking ventures, their independent spirit can launch them into entrepreneurial endeavors in which they can excel.

The Partner for Aries Sun and Venus

Despite your fiery nature and tendency to go after what you want in partnerships, you seek balance. To offset your quickness and drive, you thrive in partnerships that value reciprocity and with those who have an easy ability to keep their cool. Someone who lends patience, perspective, and tact will prove to be a complementary partner for Aries energy. You benefit from partners who also help you stay grounded to the earth, enjoying life's simple pleasures—and this could include culinary adventures or being in a nourishing environment that feels good. These qualities might be best exemplified in air and earth sign partners. A long-term partner for Aries will honor their need for independence and be comfortable focusing on their own creative projects or personal endeavors. When stressed, Aries might become somewhat impatient or bossy, and they benefit from forgiving, laid-back partners.

Shadow Work for Aries

The Shadow Traits: Aggression, Burnout
The Evolved Traits: Chill, Focus

The Lesson

Every sign is in a process of becoming. Aries is learning to take initiative responsibly and how to lead through developing their relationship with themselves. They are learning to master peace and the art of assertion without war. For them, knowledge of the self might take precedence over fueling balance in partnerships.

The Advice

Feelings of rage can escalate into inflammation. You require healthy outlets and benefit from direct communication—after a few deep breaths. Also, you are the initiator of the zodiac, and this means staying the course as a leader. Implementing structure into your long-term plans and finding supportive teams for collaboration will be your secret weapons for success.

The Shadow Through Tarot

While the Emperor is a trusted, capable leader in the upright position, when the Emperor is too focused on his battle scars or the power signified by his throne, he embodies the shadow side of this card—a dictator. The message of this card in the reversed position signifies an energy that is immovable, explosive, and arrogant. The reversed Emperor's volatility can be dangerous and lead to impulsivity and conflict. Taking a step back, finding humility, and witnessing the humanity in others are the lessons for the Emperor in the reverse.

Reflections for Aries

+ How can I best channel my assertive spark?
+ Is there a relationship in my life that could benefit from greater balance or a softer approach?
+ How can I show appreciation for those who support and look up to me?
+ For the sake of staying true to my own course, is there a tweak that needs to be made?

Affirmations for Aries

+ I am designed to initiate change, and I acknowledge this responsibility.
+ It is safe for me to trust my partnerships moving forward.
+ I bravely and compassionately ask for what I need from others.
+ I celebrate my inner drive and embrace collaboration as an asset.

Practices for Aries Energy

Yoga

Whether you identify as one or not, the Aries archetype is a hothead. You need a place to release all that heat and sweat it out. Also, you (and all fire signs) like to look your best and impress through your physique. Yoga will check both boxes.

Breath Work

Breath work is a great way for you to release tension. This will connect you with your emotions and help liberate pent-up feelings. It relieves stress, lowers blood pressure, and releases energy in the throat chakra. In addition to feeling lighter, a likely benefit of breath work will be improved relationships.

Active Listening

Since it's your tendency to move fast, active listening is a quick fix to avoid jumping to conclusions and saying something you'll regret later. The next time you're inclined to react rather than respond, to raise your voice or run away, take a deep breath. Hold space for the other person. Then, *decide* how to move. Active listening gives you the ability to strengthen your relationships and connects you with your inner mediator.

Utilize HALT

HALT is an acronym and tool, and it stands for "Hungry, Angry, Lonely, Tired." This is a practice of checking in with yourself around what stressors might be exacerbating the pressure in the present moment. If you're experiencing any of these, the advice is to nurture yourself by addressing the part of you that is hungry, angry, lonely, or tired. Tend to your physical and emotional needs before responding to another potential issue.

Chapter Six
Taurus

☉

Theme: The Foundation
Archetype: The Reliable Soul
Dates: April 20–May 20
Motto: "I have."
Ruling Planet: Venus
House: 2nd
Degrees: 2, 14, 26
Modality: Fixed
Element: Earth
Color: Green
Body Correlation: Throat, Neck, Thyroid
Keywords: Sensual, Stubborn, Consistent, Charming, Luxurious
Tarot Card: The Hierophant

Characters and Celebrities with Taurus Energy
+ Demeter
+ Hestia

- ✦ Julia Child
- ✦ Coco Chanel
- ✦ Audrey Hepburn
- ✦ Blanche from *The Golden Girls*

Taurus Playlist

- ✦ "Lazy Lover" by Brazilian Girls
- ✦ "Feels Good" by Tony! Toni! Toné!
- ✦ "Fashion" by David Bowie
- ✦ "Love Hangover" by Diana Ross
- ✦ "Passionfruit" by Drake
- ✦ "Red Red Wine" by Neil Diamond

Herbs and Supplements for Taurus

- ✦ Rose powder for connection to the heart
- ✦ Ashwagandha for reducing stress
- ✦ Ginger for metabolism and thyroid support

Crystals for Taurus

- ✦ Malachite for self-love and inner transformation
- ✦ Selenite for spiritual connection and aura cleansing
- ✦ Orange calcite for connecting with inner drive

In a Quote

"Happiness is in the quiet, ordinary things. A table, a chair, a book with a paper-knife stuck between the pages. And the petal falling from the rose, and the light flickering as we sit silent."

—Virginia Woolf

As a fixed earth sign, Taurus is the epitome of stability. The desire to plant roots and build a stable foundation resonates with a Taurus to their core. They are connected to the earthy, material themes of grounding and abundance. They are treasured by others for their reliability. But what is fixed earth? Concrete or an impenetrable layer of the earth's strata? When too planted, too grounded, we're left with no room to breathe and no tolerance for change. Risk becomes terrifying, and flexibility becomes a foreign concept. The continual question for Taurus is how to remain naturally grounded *while* willing to embrace evolution and inevitable life changes.

Taurus's association with beauty and luxury adds to their charm, but this is a slippery slope. On one hand, Taurus can appreciate the fruits of the earth. But if unaware, this affinity unravels into superficiality or avoidance of what's valuable. Appreciation shape-shifts into materialism. Altering Taurus's statement from "I have" to "I value" will evolve this sign. Focusing on values over possessions or allowing possessions to reflect Taurus's values liberates them.

Taurus is represented by the bull. The bull is like the ram in its ability to plow forward but will only move if his peace is challenged. The bull is very comfortable standing still. If left completely unprovoked or not compelled, he would remain immovable. The bull is doggedly stubborn, and sometimes not for the sake of defiance. He might wonder, "What's there to fight for?" If the bull isn't connected with a reason or his "why," he will remain in place.

In the Tarot

The Hierophant is the tarot card associated with Taurus. On this card, we see a figure with elaborate garb and a headpiece elevated on a throne, suggesting a position of guidance and respectability. The Hierophant depicts a spiritual teacher and is often tied to spiritual traditions and religious institutions. This is a message to seek a teacher for higher understanding and spiritual knowledge or intended as a nudge encouraging you into leadership.

It's worth noting that the Empress card is often tied to Taurus, as it is associated with Venus. The themes reflect many Taurean ideals, including connectivity to nature and the senses. The Empress is seated comfortably. Her cushioned throne is situated in a plentiful garden surrounded by tall trees, ripening corn, and flowing water. The Venus symbol prominently displayed on her rested shield signifies her connection with beauty, love, and resources. The Empress is an embodiment of feminine earthy energy.

Taurus Sun

A Taurus sun enjoys the finer things, weaving pleasure and lavishness into their daily lives. They can gravitate toward luxury brands or comfortable fabrics, and rare or gourmet foods are within their realm of interests. But financial stability is also important to them. They can hold on to a career or position that doesn't serve them and stay past their expiration date. They tend to be very loyal in their friendships and prioritize romantic partners. Known for their reliability, this is the friend you speak to after years have passed, and it's like no time has gone by. Their communication and the way they process information can be unchanging. Even the inside jokes you once shared are likely to remain the same. In committed relationships, it can be difficult for them to continue prioritizing their needs, and breakups are more difficult for them to navigate. Relinquishing control and recognizing their stubbornness is vital for their growth and evolution.

Taurus Rising

Taurus risings interact with the world through Venusian themes and process through tactile, sensory experiences. They experience life through possessions, nature, and food. Taurus risings are seen as connected to luxurious living and sensual delights, and this is evidenced through their cozy home environments. They can be financially focused and take pleasure in building wealth or managing assets. In close relationships, they may be perceived as stubborn or creatures of habit. They stand their ground through consistent action and conviction; when provoked, their partners could witness flared tempers. But with Venus as their chart ruler, they can be magnetic, and others are likely to find their company easygoing and pleasurable in general.

Taurus Moon

Taurus moons crave stability, predictability, and structure in their routine. As a result, small changes can be tough for them, and they can experience life lessons around surrender throughout their lives. In relationships, they can embody a my-way-or-the-highway type of energy. A Taurus moon's coping strategies might involve food, luxury, or retail therapy. Or, for the micromanagerial Taurus, money management can become their therapy. Building routines that include sensual elements can also be valuable for them, and these could involve moments of rest or incorporating scents or essential oils into their daily rituals. Intimately connected to nature, Taurus moons recharge through their connection to the earth. They thrive in hands-on activities, especially outdoors, including gardening, farming, or painting, where their creativity can shine.

Venus in Taurus

At home in Taurus, those with Venus here feel love through Venusian themes. Food can be the way to the heart as well as spa dates and luxury gifts. It doesn't always have to be fancy, but it must feel good and pampering. Those with this placement are deeply connected to the natural world and, more than most, appreciate the gift of flowers. They are the slowest to forgive and forget and are resistant to initiate breakups in relationships.

This can be one of the most realistic placements in terms of spending—or the most frivolous. Sticking to budgets will either be second nature or necessary for growth, and remaining too stubborn to traditional spending habits could pose an obstacle as values shift or circumstances evolve. Although creatures of stable habits, when it comes to luxury, food, or pleasure, some really let loose and spend aggressively in these areas. Venus in Taurus has a love for food and may naturally meal prep or fantasize about food. Cooking can be a form of self-love or a way to their heart.

The Partner for Taurus Sun and Venus

In partnerships, Taurus offers loyalty and romance. They are devoted partners, and they seek this dependability in their significant others. They value privacy and are attracted to partners with a mysterious side. Having inside jokes, a hidden sex life, or some taboo element in partnerships could be up their alley. They value partners who are deeply in touch with their emotions, which lends depth and excitement to their practical, steady way of being. Partners who support their hobbies, bond over meals, and are ready to enjoy cozy, relaxing evenings are essential.

Shadow Work for Taurus

The Shadow Traits: Immovability, Materialism
The Evolved Traits: Innovation, Practicality

The Lesson

Taurus is learning how to stabilize and learning lessons related to their value, including monetary and personal worth. However, there will be times when they need to find their flexibility and surrender. Taurus is learning when to surrender their investment and accept the benefits of pivoting.

The Advice

Clinging too tightly to what isn't working can begin to impact your health. This can manifest as an extreme workout routine or the pendulum swinging into overindulgence. The bull will cling to and claim the small piece of earth he stands on while the world crumbles around him, not accepting that security sometimes requires change. Your rigidity will require continual check-ins around taking a leap and taking risks when necessary.

The Shadow Through Tarot

The Hierophant in the reverse is disconnected from spiritual practices or lacking in leadership. This can indicate the need to seek some adviser and gain a higher perspective on your current situation. This can also reveal a sense of inner defeat or lack of confidence to lead and guide. Focusing on issues of self-worth and incorporating practices that make you feel good and stable are advised.

Returning to the Empress and this card's connection to Taurus, the Empress in the reverse is disconnected from her abundance. This card indicates a lack of love, sensuality, or beauty. It signifies an energy depletion and can indicate a lack of resources. Restoring a sense of vitality is advised. Both cards suggest remedies found through spiritual forms of self-care as well as through connecting with nature and healing the senses.

Reflections for Taurus

+ Where in my life could I loosen the reins and allow for more flexibility?
+ How can I nourish my spiritual side?
+ What part of my routine could benefit from a little shaking up?
+ Is there a habit or thought pattern that doesn't serve me well and is overdue to be released?

Affirmations for Taurus

+ I embrace the changing of life's seasons and ride the wave into the next chapter.
+ I appreciate my deep connection with my senses.
+ I enjoy the fruits of the earth with deep gratitude.
+ I recognize stability as one of my greatest assets.

Practices for Taurus Energy

Gardening

As a Venusian-ruled earth sign, this is your wheelhouse! When outdoors, you receive a natural cleansing of your energy and a boost. This is where you can feel replenished and restored and cultivate home-grown crops and flowers you've tended with your green thumb. Your eye for beauty can be satisfied here, too.

Aerobic Exercise

We all love the Venusian associations you have with rest and relaxation, cozy dwellings, and delightful treats. But fixed earth benefits the most from air or *movement*. In addition to pushing away from any tendency to be sedentary, aerobic exercise supports a Taurus's mental health, leaving you less prone to fixating on belongings or practical matters. Movement is your medicine and a terrific tool for your processing.

Maintain Friendships When in Relationships

Fixed earth can be quite rigid in general. But you are prone to being inflexible (even if unintentionally) once you're hitched or booed up. Create the habit of reaching out to those you love. Prioritize your connections with family, friends, and freshly budding acquaintances. In addition to feeling more centered in yourself, your relationships will flourish, and your partnership can grow deeper as a result.

Expand Your Comfort Zone

As a creature of habit, intentionally pushing past your comfort zone is a great way to remain flexible and open to possibilities. To test your limits, you might consider practices like cold plunges, hot yoga, short races, or full marathons. Whichever practice you choose, this expansion can boost your self-confidence and strengthen your ability to find comfort in discomfort.

Chapter Seven
Gemini
· · · · · · · · · · · · · ·

Theme: The Alchemist
Archetype: The Intuitive Messenger
Dates: May 21–June 20
Motto: "I think."
Ruling Planet: Mercury
House: 3rd
Degrees: 3, 15, 27
Modality: Mutable
Element: Air
Color: Yellow
Body Correlation: Hands, Arms, Lungs, Respiratory and Nervous Systems
Keywords: Curious, Flexible, Communicative, Restless, Knowledgeable
Tarot Card: The Lovers

Characters and Celebrities with Gemini Energy

- ✦ Castor and Pollux
- ✦ Matilda from *Matilda*
- ✦ Gwendolyn Brooks
- ✦ Tupac Shakur
- ✦ Allen Ginsberg
- ✦ Prince

Gemini Playlist

- ✦ "Thinkin Bout You" by Frank Ocean
- ✦ "Playground Love" by Air
- ✦ "Fly Away" by Lenny Kravitz
- ✦ "I Heard It Through the Grapevine" by Marvin Gaye
- ✦ "All I Do" by Stevie Wonder
- ✦ "Bonnie and Clyde" by Brigitte Bardot and Serge Gainsbourg
- ✦ "Constant Surprises" by Little Dragon

Herbs and Supplements for Gemini

- ✦ Lion's mane for cognitive support
- ✦ Peppermint for respiratory health
- ✦ Lavender for calming the nervous system

Crystals for Gemini

- ✦ Amazonite for heart and throat chakra alignment
- ✦ Citrine for natural joy and playfulness
- ✦ Shungite for energetic shielding and EMF protection

In a Quote

"I'm a writer, and everything I write is both a confession and a struggle to understand things about myself and this world in which I live. This is what everyone's work should be—whether you dance or paint or sing.... You stumble forward, confused, and you share. If you're lucky, you learn something."

—**Arthur Miller**

Mutable air is like ether. You can't control it. You can't predict its comings and goings. If you try to hold air in your palm, it'll slip between your fingers. The messenger swoops in, delivers the message, and vanishes. Their youthful spirit, alongside mental agility, confuses most people. Gemini can cut to the truth with their words with an uncanny swiftness. Where someone assesses their options as two sides of a metaphorical coin, Gemini recognizes the coin is really a cube with triple the possibilities. As an information sponge with a knack for trivia, Gemini personifies a Rolodex of data, which stems from their curiosity, longing to understand, and desire to feel understood. They are often viewed as clever, a jack-of-all-trades, and unpredictable.

But Gemini is the airiest of air, begging for an inner check-in around how to incorporate the elements of water, fire, and earth. Gemini, how do you channel your will or desires and give them a firm, practical place to land? How do you use your insights as messages and alchemize them into the physical realm?

As one of three dual signs, Gemini is characterized by the twins. There are three of this type of sign (the others include the fellow air sign of Libra and fellow mutable sign of Pisces), and this duality lends to their complexity, allowing them to embody a split perspective. Gemini is mythologically tied to Castor and Pollux, and the symbolism of the twins highlights how Gemini can be perceived and how they view the world. The world is abundant with options and opposing outlooks. Why would Gemini not offer the vantage point that is available but overlooked? Why would Gemini take something at face value when there is an opportunity for negotiation? It isn't an internal question Gemini has to ask; it is a way of being that is intrinsic to their outlook. With their ruling planet of Mercury, the planet of communication, their multifaceted perspective is revealed through conversation and writing.

In the Tarot

The Lovers is the card associated with Gemini, and this reflects the symbolism of the twins. In it, we find two people reminiscent of Adam and Eve naked in a garden. Bright colors abound from natural elements. Balance is suggested through the near symmetry of the card: the lovers on either side, trees growing behind each of them, a mountain centering the card, topped with an archangel and the sun overhead. This imagery suggests a balanced union that is interwoven with a spiritual theme. This card can refer to a harmonious union of two people or a unifying of masculine and feminine energies within oneself. The Lovers can also represent a choice to be made and points toward the value of external options or inner duality.

Gemini Sun

A Gemini sun looks at life as a textbook and seeks out multiple forms of learning, whether through life experience or formal study. Their desire to learn drives them, and their connections fuel this knowledge. Their multifaceted outlook gives them a rare bird's-eye view. Notice the number of times you hear "I think" from your Gemini friends. An intelligent sign, they can be easily intrigued and just as easily bored. This boredom and swiftness can result in flightiness, moving swiftly from one person, place, or thing to the next. Originality speaks to them, and concepts that go against the tide will arouse their interest. This is a highly creative placement with a lengthy roster of celebrity artists, including Prince, Tupac, and Stevie Nicks. They appreciate working with other creatives and sharing their original ideas. In work, Gemini suns are either skilled at multitasking or overwhelmed by multiple responsibilities. They may oscillate between these positions.

A Gemini sun is capable of quickness and known for fun, but at their core, they have a depth to uncover. With easy-to-access humor and playfulness, they must be careful of others mistaking their child-like nature for childish naivete. They reconnect with their sense of self through play and activities they enjoyed in childhood.

Gemini Rising

A Gemini ascendant views the world through a lens of immense curiosity. They are adventurous and learn life lessons through their fearlessness and willingness to take risks. Each of the air signs moves swiftly—particularly Gemini. Gemini risings are on a mission to collect data. It's as though information is a life force and tied to deep meaning. Their ruling planet, speedy Mercury, keeps them moving quickly. Building relationships with people from all walks of life and living in cities can best suit their cravings for connection and stimulation.

Gemini risings often dress gender-neutral and can appear gender-fluid. A natural social butterfly, they have eclectic social circles that tend to be filled with acquaintances. In conversations, they ask off-the-wall questions that provoke head turns and deeper probing. In an optimistic, high-energy scene in the *Barbie* movie, Barbie asks, "Do you guys ever think about dying?" This random bout of inappropriateness is peak Gemini behavior. When people need to see a new angle on an existing situation, a Gemini ascendant can lend a new perspective. As a jack-of-all-trades placement, Gemini risings can be perceived as knowledgeable but scattered in their work or distracted in life. The key for them is to assemble their knowledge and use it effectively. Focus is key to their success.

Gemini Moon

A Gemini moon needs to understand feelings; the route to their heart and intimacy is mental clarity. Anything that disrupts their mental clarity is an anti-love language, making them the least tolerant moon sign for mind games or lying. A Gemini moon can be fickle in their mood, flip-flopping in their emotions and making decisions on a whim. Like Gemini sun and rising, they can be easily distracted and move briskly between tasks. They are prone to exploring digital rabbit holes, keeping many browser tabs open, and engaging across social media platforms. They are best served by taking their time before acting and communicating their feelings.

They tend to grasp *concepts* surrounding their feelings without *feeling* and transmuting their feelings. It will benefit them to sink into their heart, exploring and transmuting their emotions. One of the healthiest forms of processing for Gemini moons is writing.

Venus in Gemini

For Venus in Gemini, love can be found through the mind, and catering to their curiosity can be a key to their heart. They thrive on mental connectivity and appreciate the flexibility to zoom from topic to topic in conversations. Similar to their knowledge counterpart, Sagittarius, they may invest in experiences that satisfy their curiosity, and purchases related to education or books are their budget's kryptonite. Financially, Venus in Gemini benefits from greater intentionality in spending and budgeting. They can be flighty in love and spending habits—and quick to change their mind and invest elsewhere—especially during their younger years. There can also be high unpredictability in their partners and whom they choose as love interests. They can be hard to pin down or to control.

They tend to have a quirky sense of style, melding different fabrics, colors, and eras into their wardrobe. Sometimes, their dress can be androgynous with interwoven sultry feminine and playful boyish elements. They tend to embrace phases with fashion or their sense of style throughout their lives. In photographs, they favor one side of their face.

The Partner for Gemini Sun and Venus

Gemini's match will be optimistic, choosing to see life's glasses as half-full. A long-term partner will appreciate their curiosity for life and desire to learn. Being an expert in their field or a frequently stamped passport holder will be an instant turn-on, but a stable, achievement focused partner will best complement them. It's important that their partner communicates well, and cleverness and a broad vocabulary are bonuses. Within the confines of commitment, the right one will leave them feeling free and understood. A natural networker and social butterfly, Gemini may need a partner capable of flying alongside them. Great conversations, genuine curiosity, and fun experiences are keys to Gemini's heart and mind.

Shadow Work for Gemini

The Shadow Traits: Fickle, Impulsive
The Evolved Traits: Wise, Intentional

The Lesson

For Gemini, movement comes easily. Mental gymnastics can be a sport, and you can use your agility in beneficial ways. But controlling the mind and its wanderings and remaining focused are your life lessons.

The Advice

Be here now. One by-product of a mind that runs a million miles a minute is a flighty attention span. There's benefit to soothing the frenetic nature of your ruling planet, Mercury, and of all the signs, you benefit the most from present-moment awareness exercises. Make the intentional choice to devote your energy where you are most curious and to the path that aligns with your desires. This conscious decision-making will not only calm your mind and nervous system but will also be key to your success.

The Shadow Through Tarot

The Lovers card in the reverse can indicate a standstill or feeling stuck in decision-making. It can signify that through inaction and lack of intention, a less ideal path is being formed for us. As the imagery and name suggest, this card can also indicate disconnection in partnership or a feeling of inner disharmony. It can reveal a communication breakdown, and this can be resolved through gaining clarity. If you must make a decision, clarify what you want so that when the time is right, you can choose according to your needs. In matters of the heart, your words could play an integral role in healing a connection.

Reflections for Gemini

+ Which area of my life would benefit from greater structure?
+ What practices in my routine help me feel grounded?

+ In the upcoming week, where might I need a renewed focus of my energy?
+ Is there an area of my life that could benefit from a little slower pace?

Affirmations for Gemini

+ I align my mental abilities with the passion of my soul.
+ I quiet the opinions of others.
+ I celebrate my unique gifts and natural curiosity.
+ I look for practical ways to ground my ideas in tangible projects.

Practices for Gemini Energy

Work with Microsteps

Mercury, your ruling planet, is the fastest planet. While this can work to your benefit, as the winged messenger, you'll need to pin down your goals. Essentially, you want to avoid the trap of being scattered and half completing tasks—especially ones that mean a lot to you. Ground your goals by taking one step at a time toward them. These are microsteps, or microgoals. No major leaps are necessary here. And as they take shape and adjustments become required, you'll adapt nicely.

Don't Overpromise

Just because you move fast doesn't mean you can accomplish it all. This includes your responsibilities *and* the desires of others. People are propelled by and feed off your energy. You are a manifester. Can you channel that juicy energy into your projects, bringing thought to form? And where can you underpromise to achieve or create what you want?

Regularly Journal

So many thoughts, so little time! You thrive on getting your ideas out into the world. At bare minimum, you can lighten your load by getting them down. But that doesn't require another ear or a sounding board to make it happen. Release the thoughts on paper. You'll feel better.

Share Your Feelings

Your gifts lie in communication, and often, your perspective is nuanced. While it requires vulnerability to go emotionally deep and let it out, it's much better than the alternative route of keeping content in your mind. Share your feelings in your platonic and romantic relationships. This will deepen your connections, and like the benefits of journaling, you'll allow the energy to be released instead of pent up.

Chapter Eight
Cancer

Theme: The Tender Crab
Archetype: The Mother
Dates: June 21–July 22
Motto: "I feel."
Ruling Planet: The Moon
House: 4th
Degrees: 4, 16, 28
Modality: Cardinal
Element: Water
Colors: White, Silver
Body Correlation: Chest, Breasts, Stomach
Keywords: Sensitive, Nurturing, Intuitive, Defensive, Heart Driven
Tarot Card: The Chariot

Characters and Celebrities with Cancer Energy

+ Artemis
+ Gaia

- A Fairy Godmother
- Clair Huxtable
- Robin Williams
- Mr. Rogers

Cancer Playlist

- "Sign Your Name" by Sananda Maitreya
- "Addicted to Love" by Robert Palmer
- "Seabird" by Alessi Brothers
- "While My Guitar Gently Weeps" by The Beatles
- "Just Like Water" by Ms. Lauryn Hill
- "Summertime Sadness" by Lana Del Rey
- "Simply Beautiful" by Al Green

Herbs and Supplements for Cancer

- Lemon balm for soothing
- Milk thistle for detoxification
- Valerian for improving sleep

Crystals for Cancer

- Moonstone for connecting to nature
- Labradorite for intuitive connection
- Bloodstone for grounding and courage

In a Quote

"In my most natural state, I'll be introverted for say, six days in a row, and then on the seventh day I'll become very extroverted.... Then I'll have to go back inside myself.... It's something I can't really control. It's a bit like the ocean and the tides."

—Björk

As the first water sign, there's a tenderness and fragility surrounding Cancer—as well as the crab symbolizing it. Life isn't all scary. But to the crab washed along the shore at the whim of the tide, it can feel that way. When you're used to the sea, the water can override the other elements. If tucked away for too long, those feelings might erupt into a tidal wave. Cancer's gift, as well as their kryptonite, is their capacity for emotional depth, and as a cardinal water sign, Cancer is learning to navigate feelings.

Ruled by the moon—representing maternal energy and sitting opposite paternal energy in Capricorn—Cancer is a part of the axis that represents parental figures. This can express itself through a range that includes nurturing, loving, controlling, or detaching emotionally. Glancing one sign before, if Gemini wants us to think how they think, Cancer wants us to feel how they feel. Cancer must be aware of their emotional regulation more than most signs, as their cardinal energy can manifest as erratic heart-over-head decision-making. Emotional regulation instead of suppression will benefit them and others as they safely navigate the shore and relationships that truly serve their well-being.

Cancers need this gentle reminder: you weren't born to hide in your shell. More importantly, Cancer, how do you remind yourself of that and not wait for someone to tap on your shell and remind you? Cancer's lifelong learning revolves around their capacity to give that reminder to themselves—and, with bravery and grounding, express their feelings.

In the Tarot

The Chariot is the tarot card for Cancer. On it, we see a figure riding a chariot led by one black sphinx and one white, equalizing the proportions of this card. Balance is a theme represented by these two figures. With a town in the distance, movement is implied, and the message is that focus and balance are necessary for forward momentum. Without it, the chariot would ride adrift and abandon any destination. The face-front positioning of the chariot's driver reminds us of the cardinal energy and the importance of moving forward with intentionality.

Cancer Sun

Cancer suns have moved from the lessons of the past three signs, including self, possessions, and ideology, into the realm of feelings. Perceived as sensitive, they are not only sensitive to their own needs, but they often intuit the needs of others. Others have the chance to learn about themselves through the Cancerian lens. As the sign associated with maternal energy, others tend to look to them for emotional support. Cancer sun's life lesson is to learn how to self-nurture and to find the balance between overwhelm and suppression. Another necessary lesson is to discern between nurturing others and serving while bypassing their own needs. Their nurturing nature is attractive, and they must be discerning of the community they cultivate. They benefit from gauging reciprocity in all of their relationships.

As the sign tied to the fourth house, their private life is one of their top priorities. They benefit from keeping their work and public life separate from their personal lives. This helps Cancer suns feel grounded and balanced.

Cancer Rising

Cancer risings understand the range found in life—its beautiful and challenging facets. They tend to be creatives or, at least, thrilled to visit a gallery, consume others' art, or take in a show. Like Cancer suns, they can experience the full gamut of emotions that others may suppress or not easily access. If they mismanage those emotions, they appear moody and may quickly make themselves emotionally unavailable to others. They connect to the world through their heart space and can interact with the world in emotionally responsive ways, manifesting as nurturing or potentially manipulative. They can be torchbearers for others' suffering and are skilled at creating a cozy atmosphere. Often, this placement wants to make sure you're well fed, not worried about basic needs, and able to sleep soundly. Cancer rising is the protector through everyday nourishment. They are natural providers, and their gauge for helping is how those around them feel.

Cancer Moon

Cancer moons are very intuitive and can be deeply connected to the dream space and their ancestry. Not only is this an emotionally sensitive placement, but they are also energetically sensitive and may identify as clairsentient or capable of detecting others' unexpressed feelings. The impacts of others' feelings and their own can make them moody. When hurt, Cancer moons tend to overthink, sulk, eat, or cry it out. They benefit from expressing their feelings and not bottling them up to keep the peace. They also must be wary of allowing their feelings to overrun their lives. Cancer moons do well to cleanse, nurture, and protect their energy. They greatly benefit from energy clearing as a part of their routine.

Venus in Cancer

Venus in Cancer connects with others through emotional availability and responds best to those who are vulnerable. This softness extends into intimacy, where they can be consumed with how their partner feels. They appreciate compliments on their devotion to the little things—those elements that make a home feel like an abode—more than most.

Their aesthetic can revolve around the desire to feel comfortable and includes cozy fabrics and fits. This is like Goldilocks finding the "just right" things throughout life. Their home is important to them, and having it feel like a sanctuary is tied to their emotional stability. Their home or workspace in disarray can reflect some internal disorder. Home aesthetics are significant and give them a sense of peace in a chaotic world. Cancer moon and Venus find grounding through decorating their space and making it feel comfortable. Home cleaning can be a source of stress relief, and you can find them doing DIY projects or reveling in building things for their home. Regardless of gender, they may lean toward pinks, soft blues, white, or pastels. They can be very protective of loved ones and sentimental in their gift giving.

Highly sensitive, this placement must be aware of emotional volatility. Venus in Cancer can be sensitive to the needs of family members and must actively prioritize their *own* needs. This placement romanticizes the past and craves knowledge of their ancestry. They tend to collect memorabilia with emotional ties to their past, and purging or clearing their space can be an emotional process.

The Partner for Cancer Sun and Venus

In partners, Cancers seek stability and appreciate partners in leadership or authority positions. With Saturn as the ruler of their partnership house, they tend to seek partners who feel like caretakers or disciplinarians—and they need to be careful not to confuse love with restriction and control. Once they question trust in their partners, they can be quick to cut them off and retreat into their shells.

They crave structure in their relationships and the freedom to be vulnerable. Like Cancer, the right partner will also gravitate toward cozy spaces and experiences, prioritizing safety and their private lives. Cancerians enjoy the process of getting to know their partners and their preferences. As a busy caretaker for everyone else, Cancer benefits the most from a partner who is reciprocal and sensitive in love, checking in on them and their needs. The right fit for Cancer will feel like home.

Shadow Work for Cancer

The Shadow Traits: Avoidance, Withdrawal
The Evolved Traits: Maturity, Directness

The Lesson

Ruled by the moon and opposite the rulership of Saturn, this is the axis of parental energies. The life lesson for you, dear Cancer, is mastering emotional regulation and learning to nurture and caretake yourself. Specifically, this will be done through maternal instincts, such as connecting with your intuition and ensuring that your emotional and physical needs are being met.

The Advice

Being tuned in to your emotional landscape is valuable, but it doesn't have to rule you. This depth and awareness makes for terrific art. Suppression is not advised, so how can you channel your deep feels? Don't sit alone on the couch. Don't masochistically dissolve from the difficult sensations. Does it just need to be spoken from the heart? Stand. Speak. Use that cardinal energy and express it.

The Shadow Through Tarot

The Chariot in the reverse indicates a lack of direction. As a cardinal sign, you will be tasked with taking initiative for yourself and others. When this card is reversed, there can be a need for clarity before moving forward. This card in reverse can also indicate stubbornness and the need to surrender to a new direction. Sometimes, the answer lies in moving off course and onto a new, purposeful path. When you're unsure of the next step, moving along a trajectory that is aligned with your values will be key.

Reflections for Cancer

+ Where might I be outsourcing my power? Specifically, where might I be outsourcing my power to gain someone else's approval?
+ Where do I need to detach for my highest good?
+ What healthy practices do I rely upon when I am tempted to ruminate?
+ Is there an area of my life that might benefit from a little bit more risk-taking?

Affirmations for Cancer

+ I have the emotional resources inside of myself that help me feel good and execute self-mastery.
+ I take responsibility for nurturing myself as a top priority.
+ I use my intuitive awareness in ways that serve my practical life and help me to move forward.
+ I recognize regulating my emotions is my responsibility, and others are responsible for their emotional landscape.

Practices for Cancer Energy
Create a Nurturing Morning and Nightly Routine

These practices will cater to your desire to feel good while keeping you away from ruminating and unproductive thoughts. Because as much as you are a sign of feeling, your hidden shadow is your ability to dwell. Channel that energy into your nurturing and do it for *yourself*. Make a schedule out of it—and have fun!

Budget

I know. This one isn't cute or cuddly. But sharing your axis is Capricorn—strategic, plotting, and money driven. This opposing energy indicates that this is something you value in others and, specifically, in your partners. One of the most hidden ways for you to feel nourished is to cultivate good money habits for yourself. This is also a beautiful diversion from the watery depths you are drawn into—which is not a bad place to be. But budgeting will help you feel like a secure crab rather than one tossed along the shore.

Cultivate Your Creative Practice

You have hidden talents that make your heart happy. Plus, creating helps you positively connect with your emotions. While you're creating that nourishing morning and evening routine, fold in time for your art, hobbies, or crafts. Don't allow your gifts to languish or your light to fade. You don't have to be ready to share your creations with the world in order to foster your talents.

Don't Avoid Conflict

When emotions feel overwhelming, there can be a tendency to retreat into your shell. Or you can tend to bottle those feelings up and overreact on a future date. For the health of your relationships and honoring of your feelings, don't bolt when the going gets tough. This helps to prevent reactions that are disproportionate in the future, too. Express yourself.

Chapter Nine
Leo

Leo symbol ♌

Theme: The Brazen Sun
Archetype: The Celebrity
Dates: July 23–August 22
Motto: "I will."
Ruling Planet: The Sun
House: 5th
Degrees: 5, 17, 29
Modality: Fixed
Element: Fire
Color: Gold
Body Correlation: Heart, Spinal Column, Upper Back
Keywords: Proud, Charismatic, Playful, Courageous, Creative
Tarot Card: Strength

Characters and Celebrities with Leo Energy
+ Zeus
+ Cleopatra

- Madonna
- Mick Jagger
- Gisele Bündchen
- Arnold Schwarzenegger

Leo Playlist

- "Diva" by Beyoncé
- "I Feel Love" by Donna Summer
- "Good Time" by Brazilian Girls
- "Glow" by Kelis and Raphael Saadiq
- "Deeper and Deeper" by Madonna
- "Young Hearts Run Free" by Candi Staton

Herbs and Supplements for Leo

- Orange blossom or cinnamon for invigoration
- Schisandra for heart connectivity
- Saffron for connection to the sacral

Crystals for Leo

- Sunstone for connecting with your inner nature and joy
- Tigereye to support your drive and creativity
- Rose quartz for self-love and compassion

In a Quote

"Being a star just means that you just find your own special place and that you shine where you are. To me, that's what being a star means."

—Dolly Parton

When you're born for the spotlight, it might feel a little challenging for others to relate to you. Ruled by the sun, Leo's radiant energy fuels their natural inclination for center stage. Their connection with their inner child is important, and this manifests through their spunk, playfulness, and courage to express themselves. Their heart space is large, but their feelings can be overshadowed by bravado or their desire to keep things light and jovial. That bravado can make them an easy target for the projections of the less confident, who might miss the warmth and openness of Leo's heart. Extending their exuberance to those missing their spark can have a tremendous impact. Leo, since the shine is effortless, how can you hold up a mirror for someone struggling to see their own light? How can your magnetism become a gift that serves another?

In grandiose fashion, the lion is the symbol of Leo. You can't miss a lion. Courageous and eye-catching, the lion represents the Leo confidence and presence that launches them into the center of attention. Lions embody tremendous strength, and after that first fearful impression of them, their lionhearted courage is renowned.

In the Tarot

Leo's card in the tarot is the Strength card. A woman is depicted holding shut the mouth of a wild lion. Their relationship appears gentle and pleasant. The dynamic provokes questions—as creatures, are they really so different? Has she tamed a perceived beast, or has she connected with him through love? And are these both aspects of one individual? An infinity symbol above her head brings a spiritual element to the earthbound illustration and implies her connection to the expansive Universe. The Strength card invites us to summon the courage for what we perceive to be an impossible task.

Dominated by the colors yellow and orange, associated with the sacral and solar plexus chakras, this card connects with drive, creativity, and personal will. These are the themes of Leo energy, and cultivating a healthy sense of drive, allotting space to create, and aligning will with intentionality are the path toward Leo's greatest gains.

Leo Sun

As the sign ruled by the sun, Leo suns are the embodiment of center stage. They tend to have no trouble lighting up a room or leading a conversation. They set an example for others on how to take up space. In their most balanced and healthy embodiment, they are confident and express themselves well. This expression will come naturally to them, and they can be unapologetic about it. When immature, they might dominate. No matter the state of maturity, allowing others to take up space and nudging them into the spotlight can be an act of service or good deed for Leo suns—and this could feel like shrinking themselves down. Leo suns also tend to make terrific performers, and this is a highly creative placement. They are great at leading groups, setting artistic standards, and breaking the ice with their splendid sense of humor. Appearance is important to Leo suns. They can be emotionally connected to their hair, or lion's mane. Doing things that align with their heart, no matter how childlike their actions appear, is essential for their vitality. In their professional lives, they can easily find themselves in leadership positions in the entertainment or fashion industries or mentoring others. They crave authentic connections, heart-to-heart conversations, and playful ventures with their inner circle. They tend to feel most comfortable surrounded by trailblazers, innovators, and fellow creatives.

Leo Rising

Like Leo suns, Leo risings can feel magnetized toward the limelight and positions where they will be seen. Regardless of their physical appearance, people can be naturally attracted to them. They can easily step into leadership roles, and when they take to the stage, people listen. Since this magnetism is inherent, preparation and aligned opportunities are all they need. Leo risings are best served by having a clear focus and mental preparation so that they can step forward with ease and effectiveness when the timing is right. At times, they can have a domineering lean in partnerships, and they benefit from ensuring partners feel seen and heard.

This placement has great leadership ability and can give noteworthy speeches and confidently address groups. With a natural celebrity quality to them, they can go far by taking their private lives and reputations seriously—so that the spotlight doesn't emphasize things they'd prefer to be kept unseen. Leo risings can embody bravado, pride, or courage and be the life of a party.

Leo Moon

Leo moons are bold and courageous in matters of the heart. As the sign associated with the heart, Leo moons are all-in in their relationships. Their affection is large, and their love language can involve public declarations or displays—either receiving or giving them. They can also have a flair for the dramatic and be confident in their self-expression. Their feelings, wardrobe, and creativity can be inextricably linked—Leo moons self-soothe by connecting to their confidence, joy, and creativity. Doing activities for pleasure, with no reward or purpose, can be stress reducing, and any activity where they get to shine can reacquaint them with their self-assurance. Leo moons thrive on connection. They long to feel appreciated for their childlike spunk and self-expression. They benefit from sharing themselves, their projects, and what excites them, but they elevate or mature by not over-relying on validation through their connections. Connecting with their inner child is healing for Leo moons.

Venus in Leo

Similar to Leo sun and ascendant placements, Venus in Leo can be very connected to personal appearance and aesthetics. The art of dressing can resemble a fashion show. Unique flair, eccentric accents, and bold colors are all in the realm of Venus in Leo. They can be very connected to their hair, which may take on the silhouette of a lion's mane. In their dress, they typically gravitate toward bright colors and metallics reflecting their natural radiance. Their home décor reflects the flair for the dramatic with bold textures and colors, and they incorporate decorative accents from different periods or eras.

In love, there is no such thing as too much attention for this placement. They want to feel adored but believe strongly in reciprocity and will return the love. They swoon over big, bold gestures in love. The musical theater number involving an outpouring of love and breaking into song will surely hit the jugular when directed toward them. But it's not all things superficial for this placement. Connected to their heart, they do sense genuine outpours versus casual fluff. They are moved by and invest in the real thing. They can be sexually curious, open, and even theatrical.

Venus in Leo is comfortable as the center of attention. They appreciate striking experiences and faraway trips. They don't have to be the most luxurious, but they're usually visually stunning and must be fun. This placement thrives off genuine good times and belly laughs. They appreciate a group of friends who are in alignment with their silly, fun nature and have a playful sense of adventure. They may make big purchases, especially ones tied to these experiences, but they aren't usually frivolous or obsessed with money. Their joy is worth more to them. They enjoy seeing others' happiness and will use their playfulness to spark joy in others.

The Partner for Leo Sun and Venus

Despite being a fixed sign, you can handle the curveballs, and your ideal partner will keep you on your toes. A partner who ignites your innate passion and lets you feel comfortable in your charisma, free from judgment, is a keeper. Without too much pressure, they might nudge you out of your comfort zone and will appreciate your enthusiasm for life. Your match will recognize your regal qualities and value, and you will likely enjoy celebrating these attributes in your partner. Your partner will celebrate your desire to perform and not be intimidated by the attention you receive. Self-assurance is a must in Leo's partner; to them, confidence is one of the sexiest attributes. As a fixed fire sign, Leo is ferociously devoted to those they love and needs their steadfastness reciprocated by their mates. Grounded and levelheaded attributes are some of the most complementary qualities to balance Leo's bravado and joie de vivre.

Shadow Work for Leo

The Shadow Traits: Self-Absorption, Triviality
The Evolved Traits: Empowerment, Purpose

The Lesson

As the sign associated with the statement "I will," Leo is learning to connect with their willpower or inner strength and take the lead in their life. But since you share an axis and life lessons with Aquarius, your lesson also revolves around discernment with your energy.

When is it best to share your light for the sake of a group or cause? You are learning how to let your shine radiate in a way that benefits more than just yourself.

The Advice

When you live out of alignment with your joy, your fire diminishes to a spark. Your joy is your fuel. It's also no one's responsibility to find it for you or bring it out of you. Engage in the activities that make you feel most alive. Connect with those who share your passion and love for life. Then, just be you.

The Shadow Through Tarot

The Strength card in the reverse leaves the woman and lion on their heads, indicating a lack of confidence and a need for grounding. It suggests disconnection and stubbornness. Connecting with your personal willpower and discovering inner strength are necessary for healing. You might also need to see something from a renewed or higher perspective. The infinity symbol on this card highlights the spiritual connection as a means for gathering courage and returning to the essence of yourself.

Reflections for Leo

+ Which relationship in my life could benefit from my love and attention?
+ Which humanitarian cause am I most passionate about promoting?
+ What's a nostalgic activity that I can revisit?
+ Could my routine benefit from a genuine self-care practice?

Affirmations for Leo

+ I align my superpower of embracing the spotlight with my passion and purpose for others.
+ I tend to my heart, acknowledging it as the source of my strength.
+ Acknowledging that magnetism carries responsibility, I take accountability for my words and actions.
+ I prioritize my joy intentionally through rituals.

Practices for Leo Energy

Book a Spiritual Healing Practice

An indicator of a mature Leo (one doing the inner work) is that they tap into their spiritual practice. If you routinely do this for yourself or with a practitioner, great! By using the tools in this book, you're also feeding that path. But if you're looking for a little *more* guidance, book a session for a personal tarot or astrology reading or an energy-clearing session with a practitioner who you feel is right.

Perform Acts of Service

Aquarius, the sign associated with humanitarian actions, shares your axis. In some ways, this is like your older, more evolved sibling. While you are fully encouraged to embrace your natural celebrity energy, take a cue from Aquarius and act where you feel called for a cause or underserved group. This may naturally make your heart happy.

Share Your Art

Not only are you a creative sign, but you have a capacity for courage that a lot of signs seek to emulate. Why not take all that natural pride and shine through your creative endeavors? Others benefit from your finished product, but they can also learn from witnessing your promotional skills and your ability to sparkle.

Embrace that Life Is Cyclical

Since you are ruled by the sun, high-energy and joy-filled environments can easily become your expectation. While we collectively crave joy, you may be more sensitive to discomfort or inevitable dips. Remember that life's lows and grief seasons are cyclical. These are windows of time, and joy is discoverable around the corner.

Chapter Ten
Virgo

. . . .

♍

Theme: Self-Mastery
Archetype: The Intuitive Sage
Dates: August 23–September 22
Motto: "I analyze."
Ruling Planet: Mercury
House: 6th
Degrees: 6, 18
Modality: Mutable
Element: Earth
Colors: Brown, Green
Body Correlation: Small Intestine, Digestive System, Spleen
Keywords: Mystical, Perfectionistic, Methodical, Brilliant,
    Restorative
Tarot Card: The Hermit

Characters and Celebrities with Virgo Energy

+ Astraea
+ Persephone
+ Nicholas Culpeper
+ Idris Elba
+ Misty Copeland
+ Marie Curie

Virgo Playlist

+ "(I Can't Get No) Satisfaction" by The Rolling Stones
+ "Girl You Need a Change of Mind" by Eddie Kendricks
+ "Perfect" by The Smashing Pumpkins
+ "Witchy Woman" by Eagles
+ "Rhiannon" by Fleetwood Mac
+ "Mental Picture" by Jon Secada

Herbs and Supplements for Virgo

+ Gingko for cognitive support
+ Sage for clearing energy
+ Passionflower for calming worry

Crystals for Virgo

+ Jade for connecting to your heart
+ Blue kyanite for activating your voice
+ Black tourmaline for protection

In a Quote

"I'm very attached to certain forms, little compulsive rituals. I like to cook; I like to sew. They're peaceful things, and they're an expression of caring."

—Joan Didion

With Virgo, we arrive at the last sign of individuality before we proceed to Libra, the sign of partnership. For Virgo, the sign of self-mastery, the bar is set high. Virgo can teeter between exquisite awareness of their healing gifts and crippling self-doubt. The wise sage is a blessing to those who know them. But pointing their word, or their wand, toward themselves with criticism defeats their natural capacity to be a healing presence. Since alchemy is driven by intention, Virgo should be clear in their aim before serving at a larger capacity. The question for Virgo is who is setting that bar, and is it imperative that it be that high? The embodied and wise Virgo will continually shift the bar for themselves in life with a goal of self-mastery combined with self-grace—because no one is harder on a Virgo than themselves.

Virgo's symbol is the maiden. She carries corn or a sheaf of wheat and is associated with the harvest and the seasonal transition of summer into fall. This symbol of harvest reminds us that she is connected to the element of earth. Virgo's association with the shifting into a new season, combined with the earth element, makes them adaptable and capable of making practical transitions and points to themes of alchemy and earth magic. Sitting across from Pisces on the healing axis of the zodiac wheel, Virgo, or the maiden, is a healer, often incorporating their gifts into their profession.

In the Tarot

The Hermit is the tarot card for Virgo. In it, we see the profile of a cloaked figure guided by the lamp that lights his path. The brightness of his light, or truth, illuminates his more solemn surroundings. His long gray beard suggests wisdom, and his walking stick reveals a long-traveled road of experience. He stands chin down in a humble pose of service, shining the light for the rest of us. This card suggests the value found through a period of seclusion for the sake of going within. It

can also reflect the wisdom that comes over time and through aging. The Hermit is an enlightened figure with knowledge to share—and we'd be wise to receive it, especially if that wisdom is discovered by seeking answers inside of ourselves instead of through an external sage.

Virgo Sun

As the sign of service, Virgo sun is a healer in the practical world. They can be natural herbalists, whipping up restorative recipes in the kitchen, naturally forming a connection between their intuition and medicinal herbs and plants. They also feel a sense of duty to serve others through their resources, time, and acts of kindness. Virgo suns proceed the sign of partnership and are learning lessons in self-mastery. As a result, they are meticulous and can be organized and critical. They must avoid harsh self-criticism, which can impact their health and relationships. Yet this is how they are so equipped to instruct others. Through self-induced hard knocks, they write the guide for everyone else. Ruled by Mercury, they are highly intelligent and, as their motto emphasizes, analytical. They are intentional with the words they choose and consider a broad vocabulary an asset. Finding their recharge in nature and connecting with the elements nourishes their soul and calms their nervous system.

Virgo Rising

Virgo risings interact with the world through analysis and critique. Their eye for detail transcends into their abode, aesthetic, work, and creative projects. They consume information quickly, processing through a lens of logic and mind over heart. They can make wonderful editors, critics, and consultants, and with a useful perspective for refinement, they offer the most constructive second opinions. Sometimes, they can appear cold or sharp in their delivery, even when their intention is improvement. Associated with the house of health and wellness, they tend to be health conscious and passionate about the quality and sources of the food they consume. Folding rituals into their day, their lives can revolve around routines that support them. In their dress, Virgo rising is typically well put together with attire that fits like a glove and nothing in disarray.

Virgo Moon

Virgo moons are natural healers. Intuitive and recharged outdoors, they feel deeply connected to nature, the elements, and animals. They are comfortable harvesting, foraging, gardening, and beautifying the planet. Virgo moons reduce stress by retreating, cleaning, learning, and researching topics that interest them. They thrive in orderly and clean environments, and organizing their surroundings helps them process emotions and feel well. In their work, they benefit from staying orderly and using their intuition. In relationships, they are highly analytical and crave conversations that are like a meeting of the minds. The way to a Virgo moon's heart is sapiosexual—through their mind. Their analytical approach serves as an insightful lens for others to see the world and offers a mature outlook. But Virgo moons must avoid trappings of the mind and being overly critical of themselves and others. They benefit from activities with friends that serve no purpose other than just having fun, which will calm their nerves and reconnect them with their joy.

Venus in Virgo

In addition to Virgo ascendants, Venus in Virgo doesn't have a hair out of place, and they have viewed themselves at all angles to ensure it. This is a very well-presented placement. Just as they can be meticulous in their appearance, they can be scrupulous in their spending, indulging in near-obsessive budgeting or penny-pinching. They can take pleasure in this control over financial matters, and this mastery of assets can be tied to their self-value. They may be critical of their spending habits or vocal about others'. They feel tied to the natural world, keeping flowers at home or folding natural elements into their wardrobe. Nature's wildness provides a contrast to their meticulousness. Tied to a sense of service, they are thoughtful in their random acts of kindness and tend to be philanthropic.

In matters of the heart, they can be very specific about whom they invest in for partners and friendships. Typically, they do not invest too much energy into large groups and will cultivate an intimate circle to confide in. They benefit from practicing vulnerability in these relationships, which will help them combat their inner perfectionism. They must avoid isolation for the sake of finding safety, as their boundaries can block more intimate connections. Like Virgo moons, they have a high bar set for their partners and are harsh on themselves when they make mistakes. Grace and a bird's-eye view, along with an occasional second opinion, serve them very well. Although often perceived as straitlaced, intimacy is crucial for Venus in Virgo, and outside of deepening connection in their relationships, it helps them feel balanced and improves their mood and well-being.

The Partner for Virgo Sun and Venus

Though you are analytical and grounded in your approach to life, in your partnerships, you can become engulfed in a dreamy, romantic fog. You must be careful not to overlook red flags and take partners at face value. A partner in tune with their spiritual side that mirrors your intuitive gifts is attractive to you and will help you feel understood, and this can be your best match. Someone with a similar eye for detail with aesthetics and dress will be attractive, but you most benefit from a partner who allows you to feel free and express the side of yourself that you hide from the world. For long-lasting romance, someone who makes you laugh and dance and helps keep your nerves at bay is a suitable counterpart. Your partner must also appreciate a tidy environment and your penchant for cleanliness and hospitality.

Shadow Work for Virgo

The Shadow Traits: Perfectionism, Avoidance
The Evolved Traits: Acceptance, Connection

The Lesson

As the sign paving the way for partnership, Virgo is associated with mastery of the self and service. Meticulous and mutable, you tend to mold yourself as you embody greater self-awareness. The task for you is resisting the tendencies to turn the analytical mind into a severe critic—of yourself or others. It suits you to learn this delineation so that self-mastery doesn't become self-punishment.

The Advice

Gastrointestinal issues and anxiety manifest from withholding your truth or staying in associations that aren't healthy for you. There is a direct connection between your feelings and abdominal discomfort, which can be used as a gauge to change dynamics in your relationships. Release the need to control how you're viewed or how some difficult conversation will unfold. Say the thing that's pent up and release any desire to control the outcome. You are already enough, and any harsh self-criticism should be uprooted. No one is perfect, and that is more than okay.

The Shadow Through Tarot

When the wise Hermit is in the reverse, his light is upside down. This indicates a lack of clarity and an inability to analyze—the task Virgo is here to execute. This can also emphasize a need to isolate for the sake of gaining wisdom. When this card is in reverse, taking time out and reconnecting with inner wisdom can be the medicine. On the other hand, this can indicate that isolation or independence isn't serving you. Instead of suppressing your needs, voice them and practice vulnerability in your relationships. Take all that wisdom learned in solitude and bring it out into the world.

Reflections for Virgo

+ How can I incorporate more acts reflecting self-compassion into my routine?
+ What intention can I set around my spiritual practice?
+ Is there a relationship that could benefit from a change in my perspective?
+ How can I activate my creative side more?

Affirmations for Virgo

+ I am enough as I am.
+ No accomplishment is a measure of my value.
+ My healing gifts benefit others, and I am worthy of sharing them.
+ I embrace the necessity of playfulness for living well.

Practices for Virgo Energy

Meditate

You share the axis of spirituality with Pisces. Meditation has two benefits for you. First, it helps you ground and stay out of any mental ping-ponging. Second, it helps you to cultivate your spiritual practice and healthily turn within yourself, benefiting your life in many ways.

Share Your Healing Gifts

You likely have information to share that benefits others. You'll know how your healing gifts apply in your life, and you don't have to deliver them perfectly. As a Mercury-ruled sign, you are dominated by the mind, and sometimes, the healing is found just through your words. Use your healing gifts to teach others, and you'll be a natural force for good in the world.

Practice Grace toward Yourself

You may be aware that you are your sharpest critic. With specific taste and an affinity for details, your precise approach can run the risk of rigid scrutiny, and this may impact your self-esteem. Along the journey, be gentle and gracious with yourself.

Dance

Underneath your polished, immaculate exterior, you have a pent-up desire to let loose. But some environments you cultivate don't allow you to let go. It's as though you have this alter ego that just wants to throw caution to the wind and have fun, and most of the time, you don't feel liberated enough. You *need* ways to do this. Since dancing requires you to let go, this is a secret joy for most Virgos. Just do it.

Chapter Eleven
Líbra

· · · · · · · · · ·

Theme: The Balanced Partnership
Archetype: The Diplomat
Dates: September 23–October 22
Motto: "I balance."
Ruling Planet: Venus
House: 7th
Degrees: 7, 19
Modality: Cardinal
Element: Air
Colors: Pink, Light Blue
Body Correlation: Kidneys; Hormonal, Lymphatic, and Endocrine Systems
Keywords: Equitable, Compassionate, Indecisive, Charming, Direct
Tarot Card: Justice

Characters and Celebrities with Libra Energy

+ Themis
+ Mahatma Gandhi

- Ruth Bader Ginsburg
- Brigitte Bardot
- Gwen Stefani
- John Lennon

Libra Playlist

- "Your Smile" by Rufus and Chaka Khan
- "War" by Edwin Starr
- "Sweet Love" by Anita Baker
- "Heart of Glass" by Blondie
- "The Way You Look Tonight" by Frank Sinatra
- "Les Fleurs" by Minnie Riperton

Herbs and Supplements for Libra

- Cacao for heart connectivity
- Goji berries for healthy skin and immune support
- Cranberry for kidney support

Crystals for Libra

- Blue lace agate for inner peace
- Amethyst for divine connection
- Sodalite for discernment and decision-making

In a Quote

"Balance is not something you find; it's something you create."

—Jana Kingsford

As a Venus-ruled sign, Libra is attached to magnetism, sensuality, and earthly delights. But it's not all light or superficial. As cardinal air, the mind can be used for strategy. Libra sits in opposition to fiery

Aries, and Libra, the diplomat, understands that the art of war is really about achieving peace. Peace overrides all. Or, in Libra's most shadowy embodiment, the illusion of peace overrides all. If balancing the scales is the most important thing, the questions for Libra revolve around integrity. Libra, how are you willing to keep the peace, and at what cost? What battles or beliefs are worth the fight? When does an illusion of harmony override moral integrity and your inner compass—or when does peace morph into people-pleasing? The answers to these questions determine the side of the scale (shadow or evolved) in which Libra resides. Libra is one of the dual signs, and each decision they face is an opportunity to choose fairness or abandon it.

Balanced partnership, fairness, and equality are all emphasized through Libra's symbol of the scales. Libra has the only symbol that is an inanimate object. The scales denote themes of objectivity and justice. In Libra's highest embodiment, we witness decisive justice without personal agendas or emotional reactivity.

In the Tarot

Fitting for the sign of the scales, the tarot card for Libra is the Justice card. In it, we see a figure sitting on a throne of stone. He holds a set of scales in his left hand and an upright sword in his right. The sword is in a position of readiness for use and in the upright is a symbol of truth in the tarot. Libra, as represented by the Justice card, is devoted to the cause of fairness. Outside of legal scenarios, this card represents cosmic justice.

Libra Sun

Libra suns are natural diplomats. They tend to be personable and are invested in their appearance through stylistic choices and accessories. They tend to communicate precisely and fairly and offer new perspectives in their collaborations. Being a cardinal air sign, they deliver insight and can initiate movements through their thoughts that others can develop into full-fledged concepts. This lens benefits them in positions of leadership or in any line of work that requires attention to detail. When working in alignment with their visionary gifts, they are an asset on any team and prized in their relationships. They prioritize their social circle and thrive in relationships with friends and colleagues who appreciate the beauty in life. The sneaky Achilles' heel for Libra suns is that their vantage point affords them multiple perspectives, often leading to indecision. They're here to pick a side and stand for truth, but vacillating can block them from this destiny. They benefit from cultivating their intuitive connection to guide them in making their best decisions.

Libra Rising

Libra risings can make natural negotiators, managers, or salespeople—especially in Venusian fields like luxury or the epicurean or beauty industries. They tend to be excellent representatives of companies and benefit from professions that involve socializing and public relations.

Libra risings can be the mediator that everyone wants and benefits from having. But in instances where their reputation is at stake, they benefit from choosing authenticity over saving face. Their relationships risk becoming stagnant from not wanting to disturb the peace. They benefit from not being conflict avoidant and prioritizing the truth over people-pleasing. They are here to learn how to interact with the world in ways that support fairness and justice, which requires honesty. In fashion and their home, they gravitate toward pinks, bright colors, soft pastels, and black. They crave a space that feels lush and luxurious, blended with practicality. They gravitate toward connections that expand their mind and appreciate others' viewpoints. Big-picture ideas, social justice, and joie de vivre topics are focal points in conversations.

Libra Moon

With Venus as Libra's ruler, this moon placement is deeply connected to sensuality. They're passionate about food, and you might find them interested in culinary classes or indulging in tasting menus and wine pairings. As a result of their appreciation for the finer things in life, they are artistically inclined and natural decorators with an eye for detail and great taste. Like Libra suns, they can be very indecisive. It benefits them to be intentional and clarify their desires so they don't get swept up in others' decisiveness. Libra moons self-soothe through cooking, pampering, and spending time in spas or treatments. They care deeply about their relationships, and heart-to-heart conversations can be their go-to for stress relief. They enjoy parties and group dinners, which help them establish balance in their lives. In anxious times, they can be prone to spending sprees and should avoid carelessness with their resources.

Venus in Libra

For Venus in its domicile of Libra, there is tension between indulgence and restraint, manifesting as oscillating between pleasure and practicality. They find great joy in food and have a green thumb, enjoying plants in their home and workspace. They care dearly about their appearance, and their self-expression can be closely linked to their wardrobe. They can be money focused and motivated by observing their gains. They appreciate the finer things in life but benefit from exercising restraint in spending.

In relationships, they are averse to ruffling feathers, which can lead to pleasant relationships but result in pent-up feelings. Sometimes, for the sake of diplomacy, they miss the opportunity for vulnerability. This placement makes for terrific mediators. A beautiful atmosphere is important to Venus in Libra. A hint—or a lot—of luxury is always welcome.

The Partner for Libra Sun and Venus

Libra's partner will appreciate their connection to sensuality, the finer things, and their outlook on the world. Libra and their partner will connect through the mind and sharing stimulating ideas. Libras appreciate partners inspired by life's simple pleasures and willing to indulge in them. To help them through indecision, the right partner will take the lead and have a strong sense of drive. Their partner will appreciate their delight in life's sensual treats, and although more depth is required, food is the key to Libra's heart. Their partner will enjoy the same environments that make them content—a dinner party surrounded by stimulating conversations that features exquisite food in a stylish space.

Shadow Work for Libra

The Shadow Traits: People-Pleasing, Indecision
The Evolved Traits: Courage, Autonomy

The Lesson

Becoming a conduit of justice is tied to your purpose. Throughout life, evading confrontation and silencing your perspective are the traps to avoid. Because you're Venus ruled and thrive through connections, it's easy to overprioritize what others think, and your purpose involves doing the fair and right thing—even when it's not easy or could damage your reputation.

The Advice
As a sign with so much pleasantness and magnetism, you must avoid being agreeable to a fault. What do you stand for, and what's worth defending? Don't sway or sit silently because it's easy. There's value in seeing both sides of life's trials, but what is your stance?

The Shadow Through Tarot
In the reverse, the Justice card reveals the absence of truth and fairness. The symbolism of the sword in the downright position suggests outright lies or dishonesty through omission of the truth. This card position reveals the need for justice and the scales to balance—whether this applies internally or in a relationship. It also suggests a lack of integrity, or an in-between state in a legal matter. Some energy exchange might be completely off-balance. The questions this brings up are "Where are we being dishonest with ourselves? Have we too easily trusted in a situation without looking into all the facts?"

Reflections for Libra
+ Which person in my life could benefit from my listening ear?
+ Is there a person or group that might benefit from me using my voice and taking a stand?
+ Where have I allowed another's agenda to override my own?
+ Where or with whom do I need to stand my ground?

Affirmations for Libra

+ I choose personal sovereignty over societal conditioning.
+ Regardless of others' preferences, I vocally honor my beliefs and feelings.
+ I will use my natural gifts of mediation to guide others.
+ Investing in myself enriches my partnerships and allows them to flourish.

Practices for Libra Energy

Establish Boundaries in Relationships

Venusian energy combined with the sign of partnerships can easily lead to loose boundaries. Your capacity for various perspectives can leave doors ajar for unhealthy relationships. As you grow and learn, you're best served by getting clear on your boundaries and putting them into practice. Each of your relationships will benefit from this.

Never Lie in Your Relationships

Cosmic justice is firmly attached to the life learnings of Libras. You've probably noticed how other people seem to get away with things, and you can't do the same. This is because integrity is so thematic in the life of a Libra. Libras have a high bar set, which seems to be held externally. Your life motto is "do the right thing," and this applies greatly to your words in partnerships. Since lying will catch up with you, honor your truth.

Channel Your Gifts into Worthy Causes

Your natural leaning toward diplomacy is one of your gifts. Your bird's-eye view and desire to maintain harmony are gifts you can contribute to worthy causes. Instead of *knowing* the right thing to do, consider channeling your sense of justice into *strategy*. Instead of lip service, put it into altruistic action.

Don't Default into Being the Nice Guy

As the diplomat of the zodiac, it can be stressful to deliver messages that ruffle feathers. But it can damage health and relationships to withhold the truth. With Saturn exalted in your sign, prioritizing authenticity is top priority. Be sure to honor your truth, as it should only build more solid connections. No need to be a quiet bystander; your truth is worthy of being shared.

Chapter Twelve
Scorpio

Theme: The Transforming Mystery
Archetype: The Fearless
Dates: October 23–November 21
Motto: "I transform."
Ruling Planets: Mars, Pluto
House: 8th
Degrees: 8, 20
Modality: Fixed
Element: Water
Color: Black
Body Correlation: Sexual and Reproductive Organs, Bladder, Urinary Tract
Keywords: Elusive, Intense, Deep, Secretive, Nonsuperficial
Tarot Card: Death

Characters and Celebrities with Scorpio Energy
+ The Metamorphosis of the Caterpillar into a Butterfly
+ Hades

+ Bilbo Baggins from *Lord of the Rings*
+ Walter White from *Breaking Bad*
+ Carl Jung
+ Anna Wintour
+ Björk

Scorpio Playlist

+ "Through Your Soul" by Amp Fiddler
+ "6 Underground" by Sneaker Pimps
+ "My Need" by Janet Jackson
+ "Private Eyes" by Daryl Hall and John Oates
+ "Mr. Magic (Though the Smoke)" by Amy Winehouse
+ "Season of the Witch" by Donovan
+ "Need You Tonight" by INXS

Herbs and Supplements for Scorpio

+ Hibiscus to promote circulation
+ Mucuna for mood elevation
+ Maca for aphrodisiac qualities

Crystals for Scorpio

+ Black tourmaline for grounding and protection
+ White howlite for unburdening
+ Fluorite for clarity and expression

In a Quote

"That's what artists do, that's what poets do ... we all do it. We start with something, and sometimes we destroy everything that we've made in order to get to the core place where we started from."

—Patti Smith

When it comes to deep dives into the unknown, Scorpio is fearless and succumbs to their curiosity for mysteries. When we consider this penetrative ability to explore taboo or intense topics with their secretive nature, we can begin to understand how Scorpio can be misunderstood. Their fixed modality combined with the water element translates into ice. This ice signifies the rigid or determined nature of all the fixed signs (Taurus, Leo, and Aquarius included). In particular, ice changes in dramatic ways; it is either shattered or melted. The chill reflects this sign's intensity, and ice's capacity to shift from solid to liquid is significant, too. Despite Scorpio's fixed nature, they can maneuver, and their evolution is found through this process of transmutation. The sign of rebirth understands the alchemy involved in dissolving for the sake of building back anew. Questions for Scorpio revolve around their secrecy and how their private lives contribute to their metamorphosis. Must they keep the mysteries to themselves? Can they afford to be vulnerable? Should they allow others into their internal process, letting the light in a little bit more?

Fitting for their intensity, the scorpion is their symbol. The scorpion is quiet in its approach but unafraid to sting and get their point across. You may not be able to predict when that hasty tail will strike. The nature of a defensive scorpion is also like ice—difficult to warm up to and capable of shocking the senses. Scorpio benefits from environments where they can let their guard down. They need to intentionally seek out safe connections and melt into vulnerability.

In the Tarot

As the sign of transmutation, Scorpio's tarot card is the Death card. In the unfolding dramatic scene, we see a knight of death riding on his horse. A priest appears, begging the knight for mercy, and while one figure is in his wake, in the distant corner, we see the sun rise over the horizon. While this theme of mortality is blatantly depicted, the Death card represents a metamorphosis. It can reveal the shedding of one way of being and the transmutation into a new one. But this

change is not superficial—it is a deep one. It can indicate a graduation in the school of life and a transformative new chapter.

Scorpio Sun

Although they're not an air sign, their intense thoughts can lead to mental anguish. Their wheels are always turning, and they can seem detached from the world around them. In reality, they're engulfed in it. Fearless and obsessive, they can go down Google wormholes and into conversational depths around psychology, trauma, and the afterlife. If you find yourself in their inner circle, you will feel like you can share anything and no topic feels off limits. Scorpio suns are playful with their inner circle. They are more sensitive than others perceive. They benefit from communication over reclusiveness and letting their partners in on their process. They are passionate in their relationships and life in general, and when something isn't working, they can be quick to cut ties. Throughout their lives, they can go through multiple deep inner transmutations, and their physical appearance tends to reflect this evolution. During those times, they benefit from a supportive mentor or therapist for sound counsel and emotional healing.

They have a mysterious magnetism to them that others find intriguing or misjudge. There is a natural authenticity to Scorpio suns, which is usually why they are so selective with their inner circle. Their bluntness tends to cut through inauthenticity.

Scorpio Rising

Scorpio risings interact with the world through deep probing, and they feel the urge to understand psychological inner worlds. In their quest for information, they are selective in their interests but obsessive once they've discovered their target. They aren't afraid to question the status quo and investigate tough questions. In relationships, they tend to hide their feelings, leading to inner conflict. To others, they seem to make abrupt decisions and 180-degree turns, but these choices result from their pent-up hidden feelings. For some, their intensity can lead to power struggles. The desire to achieve the objective, project, or title of their yearning can foster imbalances in their energy or relationships. This intensity can also lead to great achievements in their careers.

Scorpio risings usually go through a phase where they favor a dark and intense aesthetic, including burgundy, navy, or black. Sometimes, their homes take on this gothic-leaning aesthetic as well. They tend to favor one side of their face in pictures and may reveal just part of themselves in shared pictures.

Scorpio Moon

Scorpio moons value privacy. They keep firm boundaries and pieces of life tight-lipped. It's important that they only share once they feel ready and safe. They benefit from establishing relationships where they can be themselves. They are emotional deep divers, making it difficult to form intimate connections with those who aren't venturing into these depths. Authenticity is among their highest relationship priorities, and fakeness feels like kryptonite. When hurt, the ineffective road to self-soothing is rumination, mirroring Cancer placements, and they feel strongly about injustice in relationships. Scorpio moons desire to grasp the psychology behind human behavior. They benefit from speaking their feelings and cultivating their vulnerability to feel secure in partnerships and develop intimacy. They also benefit from processing feelings in a productive way, such as journaling, creating artwork, or through therapy. Scorpio moons find liberation through the transmutation of their feelings, but this can be an arduous journey requiring the surrender of obsession or control. Through processing, they can connect to a deep reservoir of personal power and change their circumstances. Scorpio is a fixed sign, meaning this change can take time, but the results will be anything but superficial.

Venus in Scorpio

For Venus in Scorpio, their partner's ability to embark into psychological realms will pique their interest. They are sensitive, intriguing, and mysterious, and these qualities can attract an assortment of people into their lives. Their partners should be aware that with this sensitivity and intrigue, those with Venus in Scorpio are learning the art of sharing themselves. They are learning not to become fixed water, or ice, as a defense mechanism. They are learning not to sting with their tail, which is quick to whip around at offenses. But they are, like the rest of us, learning. This placement benefits from responding instead of reacting when hurt or offended.

In finances, Venus in Scorpio can be emotionally ruled, and spending can become a power move. They can invest in luxury brands or a purchase that impresses others but is more tied to their sense of self. Scorpio is the sign associated with sex, and Venus and Mars in

Scorpio are highly sensual placements. Intimacy can become a means of transformation and of feeling renewed. In matters of the heart, Venus in Scorpio can take a while to open up as they are not easily vulnerable. They may hide from love or keep parts of themselves hidden to feel safe. Their music and fashion taste can be more dark or intense, and stylistically, they tend to incorporate lace, velvet, or leather into their wardrobe and décor.

The Partner for Scorpio Sun and Venus

Scorpio can be bold in love and, when they want, with expressing their deep feelings.

Scorpios value a partner who appreciates their deep probing into the intricacies and complexities of life. A partner who isn't afraid of authenticity and affords them space for themselves is important. Conversations around the psychology of human behavior, sociological musings, and deep intimacy must be comfort zones for their partner. Scorpio's partner shouldn't be freaked out by haunted houses, creepy things, or the unsolved mysteries that captivate this sign. In friendship and love, it's as though they chose you instead of you choosing them. Typically, this is a challenging sign to cozy up to, so their letting you in reveals something trustworthy within you. In younger or less evolved years, their attachment style may have been avoidant, or they seemed detached in love. For a period of their lives, they crave feeling understood while being terrified of intimacy. Once they are more mature or desire stability, they are incredibly steadfast partners capable of the gamut of playfulness to seriousness. They allow themselves to embrace their carefree and serious sides. They care greatly about their relationships, and a lifelong partner will take their career and reputation seriously. This is a sensual sign, although their desire for intimacy is more hidden than the Venus-ruled signs, Taurus and Libra. Having the lowest threshold for deception, dependability and authenticity are vital for Scorpios in their partnerships.

Shadow Work for Scorpio
The Shadow Traits: Isolation, Rigidity
The Evolved Traits: Vulnerability, Compromise

The Lesson
The theme of transmutation combined with a fixed modality lends an intense tension to Scorpio, which shapes your life lessons. You are learning how to shift and change and how to exchange energy and be in partnerships. Assessing emotional stubbornness and releasing obsession or enmeshment will benefit you and your relationships, leading you to adapt and grow.

The Advice
You are so cool, and everyone knows it. But for the sake of your freedom, can you lean into what you judge is cringe? Would your health benefit from greater authenticity in your creative expression? Instead of staring at the screen, peering in at others abandoning their self-reserved expression, find your voice and *share* it. You might surprise yourself and others with how you still make everything look cool.

Shadow Through the Tarot
The Death card in reverse indicates stagnation. This is like pressing the brakes instead of moving forward into necessary change, and it emphasizes the stubbornness of the fixed modality. There is a message of surrender here, as this card urges us to relinquish control of the status quo, or the way things currently are. Allow for the change that

is underway. Even in the reverse, the sun is still coming up over the horizon, and a new day, while different, can deliver something sweet.

Reflections for Scorpio

◆ What can I do regularly to connect with my playful side?

◆ Which new activity or hobby am I curious to try?

◆ Which practices can I incorporate to ground and nourish myself?

◆ Am I withholding my vulnerability in a particular relationship?

Affirmations for Scorpio

◆ My ability to transmute pain into wisdom is one of my greatest gifts.

◆ My capacity to dive deep is an asset and naturally aligns me with a close community.

◆ It is safe for me to love and to be seen.

◆ In my expression, I can be cringey, vulnerable, and worthy at the same time.

Practices for Scorpio Energy

Find Your Community

You are not designed to fit everywhere and mold yourself for every scenario. That is perfectly fine. Besides, you don't *really* want to fit in everywhere. But you do crave feeling understood and appreciated. You deserve an inner circle that gets you—even if that's an intimate one you trust. You are worthy of these types of connections. While others want you to drop your guard, you need a supportive community to do so.

Create a Healthy Outlet

With your secretive nature, it's common for you to repress your emotions. You need a healthy way to release them before they accumulate and you react with your Scorpionic stinger. Consider journaling or communicating your feelings through blunt conversations. Cardiovascular exercise and creative projects benefit you, too. Practices that feel good and cathartic are essential.

Speak, Don't Stalk

Your natural desire to understand, combined with your secretive nature, can have you living in the shadows and avoiding deeper levels of intimacy. In relationships, ghosting, obsession, or emotional avoidance can become a default. You will benefit from moving out of your comfort zone, which can look like avoiding rumination and expressing your feelings—even when it doesn't feel safe.

Embrace Your Spiritual Side

You are one of the alchemists of the zodiac. It serves you well to dive deep and satiate any natural curiosity toward astrology, tarot, or spiritual practices. You might find yourself more interested in psychology and shadow work, too. Lean into your mystical yearnings and explore the practices that call to you.

Chapter Thirteen
Sagittarius

Theme: The Free Spirit
Archetype: The Professor
Dates: November 22–December 21
Motto: "I understand."
Ruling Planet: Jupiter
House: 9th
Degrees: 9, 21
Modality: Mutable
Element: Fire
Color: Purple
Body Correlation: Hips, Thighs, Sacrum, Liver, Pancreas
Keywords: Adventurous, Liberated, Philosophical, Dogmatic, Optimistic
Tarot Card: Temperance

Characters and Celebrities with Sagittarius Energy
+ Chiron the Centaur
+ The Professor Archetype

+ Ludwig van Beethoven
+ Madeleine Albright
+ Toni Morrison
+ Santiago, the main character in *The Alchemist*

Sagittarius Playlist
+ "We Didn't Start the Fire" by Billy Joel
+ "Freedom! '90" by George Michael
+ "Gimme More" by Britney Spears
+ "Good Times Roll" by The Cars
+ "Do What You Want to Do" by T-Connection
+ "All Around the World" by Lisa Stansfield

Herbs and Supplements for Sagittarius
+ Dandelion for detoxification
+ Cordyceps for cognitive support
+ Frankincense for anti-inflammation

Crystals for Sagittarius
+ Charoite for spiritual connection
+ Smoky quartz for grounding and clearing energy
+ Celestite for calm and clarity

In a Quote
"Freedom lies in being bold." —**Robert Frost**

Resting on the axis of knowledge that spans between them and Gemini, Sagittarius is filled to the brim with encyclopedic knowledge. Sagittarius has graduated beyond the youthful curiosity of a student to become the scholarly professor. They are prone to instructing, allowing their expertise to overflow. They have gained their wisdom through tomes and expeditions, wise and reckless experiences. Sagittarius doesn't judge their process of attaining knowledge, which might be why they acquire so much of it. As the most grown-up fire sign, they are the bonfire and nearly impossible to manage. But this bonfire needs the earth—not only to burn brightly but as a landing place. If wild, how do they find the middle ground for themselves so they aren't extinguished or burned out? Although they are wired to become brilliant, will they discover their self-value outside their accrued wisdom?

Sagittarius's sense of adventure and their free spirit are embodied by the symbol of the archer. Focused on his aim, he looks over the horizon with his chest open to the sky. This centaur also reveals Sagittarius's fiery determination. This figure appears brave, resolute, and courageous for the fated expedition determined by where his arrow lands.

In the Tarot

Temperance is the tarot card for Sagittarius. In this comforting scene, we see an archangel pouring water from one cup into another. The angel's wings are outspread, and the crown of their head is illuminated. Surrounded by lilies and framed by a distant hilltop, the angel stands with one foot in a pool of water and one foot on the grass. Following the tumultuousness of the Death card in the Fool's journey, this angel's positioning and task at hand remind us of balance and the value of stability. With attention to feelings (water) and a sense of grounding (earth), the angel stands radiant and steadied. The Temperance card also illuminates our connection to the Divine. Temperance is one of only two cards in the major arcana (the Lovers being the other) that feature an archangel. The representation of the archangel, combined with Sagittarius's Jupiter rulership, suggests a guidance or angelic protection tied to the Sagittarian journey in this lifetime.

Sagittarius Sun

Sagittarius suns can be wild and highly unpredictable. They are driven by their instinctual need for freedom and craving for adventure, and this often leads to excursions to foreign lands. They accumulate knowledge across a broad range of topics but often become masters in their chosen field. They are intelligent, but their fun-loving nature can be their most pronounced trait. They tend to view the world as expansive and limitless with opportunities, contributing to their generous attitude and glass-half-full mentality. But when too mired in the world and lacking optimism, some can become disheartened or arrogant. It suits them well to balance a healthy dose of adventure with intentional grounding in the present moment. It also benefits Sagittarius suns to have healthy outlets to express their wisdom to those who appreciate it. Their actions reflect a sense of security and being held by the Universe. They can be optimistic in love and invest heavily in their careers—but fun must be interwoven into their work for longevity and well-being. Their optimism in life can lean toward occasional misconceptions, resulting in a detour from their intended path. But usually, nothing detrimental comes from it. For Sagittarius, the lessons along the journey are as valuable as reaching the destination.

Sagittarius Rising

Sagittarius risings are seen as hopeful, whimsical, and well educated. They move quickly and can be unpredictable. Often, they are professorial and viewed as authorities in their field. Sagittarius rising interacts with the world through a lens of luck, optimism, and movability. They love to learn and share their insights, and you will most likely find them in environments with like-minded people. Those who keep them on their toes are intriguing and life-giving for Sagittarius rising. They're likely to accept any last-minute invite for a class, seminar, or event in their field of expertise or any subject they're curious about.

They are here to learn through varied experiences, intense study, and world travel. They crave exploring the traditions of other cultures and have an affinity for learning different religions and philosophies. Over time, they tend to accumulate wisdom and teachings from various spiritual practices. They are also likely to experience another religious tradition through its spiritual practice, whether spending time in a yoga ashram, journeying to a Tibetan temple, or taking part in a plant medicine journey in Peru. Near or far, through practice and books, they are naturally drawn to experiences outside of their upbringing for their growth. They tend to be mentors for their friends and family and appreciate having their own guides for occasional wise counsel. Sagittarius suns and risings often understand more than one language.

Sagittarius Moon

Sagittarius moons value freedom and learn their greatest life lessons through their relationships. Their feelings are strongly connected to their thoughts, and intellectualizing them is a means of metabolizing emotions. A hands-on, tactile approach to learning is best for them, and they connect more deeply with themselves through connecting with others over ideas. Philosophical debates or any atmosphere that contributes to the expansion of their mind is medicine for them. Sagittarius moons relieve stress through adventure, but like Aries, they benefit from avoiding impulsivity. When stressed, they resort to work projects or a new adventure to distract them from their feelings. They tend to be optimistic, curious about the world, and students for life. Sagittarius moon enjoys historical tours and places like libraries, temples, or spiritual spaces with histories that lend them wisdom. With their affinity for faraway places, astronomy can be of interest. They can be captivated by mythology, sci-fi, or stories of otherworldly experiences.

This can be a restless placement, longing to journey and feeling FOMO from missed adventures. From the workplace to relationships and beyond, all of life is this journey. They feel emotionally connected to memorabilia from their adventures, as these are mementos signifying the connections they've formed.

Venus in Sagittarius

Similar to moon in Sagittarius, Venus in Sagittarius can be a wild child. In matters of the heart, they are blunt, eloquent, and quick to pursue their desires. Their Jupiterian lean toward positivity and expansiveness can make falling in love seem easy, and they may fall for many people throughout life. Venus in Sagittarius aligns with George Harrison's quote "I fell in love, not with anything or anybody in particular but with everything." In addition to matters of the heart, their fast, fiery nature can propel them through varied interests. But once they find their niche or commit to their partners, they tend to be all-in. Knowledge is tied to pleasure for them, and their closest relationships will be mentally stimulating. They can become natural poets, and others benefit from the tender delivery of their teachings. They are drawn to witty banter and those who expand their awareness of the world. Others are attracted to Venus in Sagittarius because of their curious hunger for life and desire to find fun in every moment.

Their thrill-seeking nature and speediness through life can extend into material matters, where spending can turn into retail therapy. They must be careful with overspending and benefit from choosing cost-effective ways to experience a sense of freedom. They love a spontaneous adventure, and their passports can be fully stamped from their immense curiosity to learn through globetrotting. They tend to decorate their homes with trinkets from their completed experiences, and their dress reflects this eclectic global flair.

The Partner for Sagittarius Sun and Venus

With Mercury ruling your house of partnerships, a curious mind and a sense of wonder are attributes of your ideal partner. Quick-moving conversations and mental agility are attractive for Sagittarius as well as a partner who is an avid reader. Someone capable of going with the flow of life and allowing you to move with that flow will be important, too. With Jupiter as your ruler, you can attract partners drawn to your optimism and general luckiness in life. If you're seeking longevity, be careful of potential partners magnetized to your expansive, lucky essence in a genie-like, transactional way. You'll need to invest with partners interested in a real, reciprocal relationship with you.

Sagittarius doesn't enjoy restriction, and for the longevity of their relationship, they will occasionally need space. The right partner for Sagittarius will appreciate their sense of adventure and be a willing companion for the unknown trails that lie ahead. Comfort found in living abroad or long-distance travel can be important for Sagittarius's counterpart.

Sagittarius stands firm in their convictions, and their partner will also appreciate the strong morals and principles that they live by. In the past, Sagittarius likely had a crush on a teacher, and their friends, colleagues, or mentors could become future romantic partners.

Shadow Work for Sagittarius
The Shadow Traits: Know-It-All-Ness, Impulsivity
The Evolved Traits: Sovereignty, Stability

The Lesson
You have lots of knowledge to share with the world, and whichever business you choose to build needs a solid foundation. Grounding is a crucial component of your evolution, but your need to feel free isn't superfluous and is necessary for your well-being. Building with those who understand your value and have complementary skills can be key to your success and contentment. Finding avenues to share your knowledge while building your foundation *and* feeling liberated will be where the magic lies for you.

The Advice
Staying the course is vital to your abundance. Be wary of allowing a temporary dream to shift you off course or cause you to abandon your path entirely. Brisk, impulsive action and finding freedom through spontaneity can be your Achilles' heel. Your knowledge and proficiencies open doors. But will you stay in the room long enough to reap the opportunities?

Shadow Through the Tarot
Temperance in the reverse has the archangel turned around, indicating a lack of grounding and feeling disconnected from the Divine or a lack of trust in universal support. The advice from this card in the reverse is to connect to your higher self or the Divine through your spiritual practices. The natural elements shown prescribe practical

advice like grounding, nature walks, or energy clearing with water, all of which are recommended when the Temperance card is in reverse.

Reflections for Sagittarius

+ What's a step I can take toward leadership and sharing my wisdom?
+ Which relationship might benefit from more childlike curiosity?
+ What is one step I can implement to add structure toward one of my goals?
+ If you're in a relationship, do you feel free to be yourself with your current partner?

Affirmations for Sagittarius

+ I lovingly share my knowledge and passion with the world.
+ No amount of expertise replaces the value of my authentic self.
+ I accept that I don't have to travel far to find my peace.
+ I can achieve grounding and liberation at the same time.

Practices for Sagittarius Energy
String It All Together
As a fire sign on the axis of knowledge, you are the scholar. You're not the entry-level teacher; you're the esteemed professor. Your wisdom is something to share and something you can profit from. But this requires connecting the dots of your experiences and seeing your wealth of knowledge for the treasure that it is. String all the pieces together and create something grand and expansive with it.

Build a Solid Foundation

Raging fire can carry you on adventures to far-flung destinations. You thrive on new experiences, which is a part of the game of life for you. But your health and well-being are best supported through stability—your mutable fire benefits from grounding. Establishing a home base, financial planning, and tethering to the present moment contribute to your long-term benefits.

Open to a New Take

Over time, with accumulated experience, you become an expert in your field. Like most of us, you become less flexible in learning and taking in new information as you mature. Take a cue from your axis counterpart and remain curious. Stay open to new takes on existing knowledge and embrace that, on occasion, it's okay to be the student.

Explore Another Country

Your inherent desires may have already pulled you to a faraway land, but you gather tremendous knowledge through long-distance voyages—and this shapes your vantage point for life. You pick up on takeaways that others might miss, and you collect data like a sponge. You may find that these journeys propel you into new hobbies or career paths, too. For you, travel is more than pretty pictures or superficial beauty. It provides you with an excitement that seems to convert to oxygen and give life.

Chapter Fourteen
Capricorn

Theme: The Material Master
Archetype: The Father
Dates: December 22–January 19
Motto: "I use."
Ruling Planet: Saturn
House: 10th
Degrees: 10, 22
Modality: Cardinal
Element: Earth
Colors: Gray, Brown
Body Correlation: Skeletal System, Including Bones and Teeth,
     Hair and Nails
Keywords: Goal Oriented, Fixated, Prominent, Authoritative,
     Determined
Tarot Card: The Devil

Characters and Celebrities with Capricorn Energy
+ Pan in Mythology
+ The CEO Role
+ A Triathlon Finalist
+ Gordon Gekko from *Wall Street*
+ Muhammad Ali
+ Tiger Woods

Capricorn Playlist
+ "Everybody Wants to Rule the World" by Tears for Fears
+ "What Goes Around" by Nas
+ "The Chain" by Fleetwood Mac
+ "Under My Thumb" by The Rolling Stones
+ "I'm Not in Love" by 10cc
+ "Ain't No Mountain High Enough" by Marvin Gaye and Tammi Terrell

Herbs and Supplements for Capricorn
+ Collagen for bone and joint health
+ Thyme for skin health
+ Arnica for anti-inflammation

Crystals for Capricorn
+ Garnet for inner connection and clarity
+ Green calcite for self-compassion
+ Clear quartz for spiritual connection

In a Quote
"I fear not the man who has practiced ten thousand kicks once, but I fear the man who has practiced one kick ten thousand times."

—Bruce Lee

As the sign of material mastery, Capricorn is highly capable and achievement oriented. Although tied to the sea goat, they embody similar inner traits to a mountain goat. Watch any mountain goat climb a near-vertical mountain, and you witness the tenacity of Capricorn. No other creature is attempting that climb. But eventually, the goat ascends to the top of the mountain. It looks down, having successfully climbed what seemed impossible, and wonders why. What did I *really* want to achieve from this tremendous climb? For the goat and the sign of material mastery, what the heart wants must stay in the viewfinder. Savoring the process outside its consequential rewards brings Capricorn into balance and soothes their inherent fixation. The question Capricorn must consider is this: Do your efforts match what you truly value?

Outside the goat's life, we see this Capricorn tenacity through the CEO or authoritative figures. With these roles comes great responsibility. And, like the goat, Capricorn takes no issue with scaling the wall. But for fulfillment's sake, they must connect with their "why." There will be instances throughout Capricorn's life that remind them that money doesn't guarantee happiness.

In the Tarot

Capricorn's tarot card is the Devil. Beneath the name and depiction lie core messages that are undeniably part of the human condition. In this card, we find two lovers bound by loose chains. Standing over them is a creature embodying characteristics of a goat, bat, and man. Though the couple resembles the carefree lovers we find in the card of Gemini, these lovers have become bound, and their energy has dulled. The two have chosen

overattachment to materialism and bondage over freedom in love. Here, the shadow themes of obsession, attachment, and toxicity are highlighted. Although the portrayal is dramatic, its message is simple. This card points to our need to detach from our desire to seek control or social status and reconnect with faith, trust, and love.

Capricorn Sun

As cardinal earth, Capricorn suns are initiating change within structures with an emphasis on efficiency and growth, which is often related to systems, structures, and finances. As we move through the archetypes, Capricorn suns are applying Sagittarius's knowledge to their practical lives and resource building. They are hardworking and natural leaders, driven by a sense of responsibility. This responsibility is important to Capricorn suns since they often assumed leadership roles at a young age. Since organization comes naturally and gives them a sense of control, managing practical matters is second nature, and they manage their lives and schedules in an orderly way. They are achievement focused and an asset in collaborations and group projects. They care deeply about others' perceptions of them. They treasure their reputation and have an obvious serious streak, but they benefit from tapping into their playful side. As the most evolved of the three earth signs, their focus on achieving a rock-solid foundation can lend to rumination and extreme investigation of its cracks—or its continual ascension. Capricorn suns approach natural setbacks and roadblocks with heavy self-criticism and inner struggle.

To those outside of their close community, they can seem emotionally avoidant or cold. To those within their inner circle, they are loyal, helping loved ones find solutions and feel supported. Within this community, they share their cloaked playful side. They tend to be secretive about spiritual matters, including their intuitive nature. The challenge for Capricorn suns is honoring their emotional needs while striving for their personal achievements. Having grace with themselves is essential, and honoring their rest has a balancing effect.

Capricorn Rising

Capricorn rising interacts with the world through the need to understand it, and they naturally manage their environments. Like Capricorn suns, this can make them great assets in teamwork or with leading groups. Capricorn suns and risings love to be surrounded by go-getters and goal-oriented achievers. They don't need the motivation, but this helps them feel understood and mirrors their determination. They are curious to grasp structures, data, and the inner workings of systems and well suited for careers involving government institutions, corporate management, and working with logistics or statistics. Lending their talents to projects, they want to build their lives, especially their careers, strategically and exponentially. Applying this control and data-based approach to their relationships can get tricky. They benefit from intentionally incorporating activities that nurture and comfort them. Soft activities like meditation, cooking, and gentle yoga balance their vigorous drive.

In their wardrobe, Capricorn risings tend to appreciate the finer things in life. They can gravitate toward designer labels, a wardrobe that makes a statement, or incorporating a bold pop of color or black. The power suit seems to have been designed for them. In their public life, Capricorn risings are always "on"—even when the spotlight isn't on them.

Capricorn Moon

Capricorn moons tend to make emotional decisions from a practical place and aligned with their long-term goals. Their feelings are tied to the material world, and sometimes, emotional spending can be a way of avoiding their feelings. They tend to make financial decisions aligned with building their reputation or career. They can be quite intuitive and choose environments where they know they make an impact. Capricorn moons self-soothe through organization, completing work tasks, and putting in effort toward their goals. They can enjoy and excel in competitive sports. As harsh self-critics, they can struggle with being self-conscious—even when perceived as assured leaders.

They may find it difficult to express their feelings, compartmentalizing them for the sake of productivity. Efficiency can make them want to *hurry and be done* with processing emotions, leading to pent-up feelings. They need to lean into their ruling planet of time, Saturn, and afford themselves patience with processing, accepting that the process of transmutation cannot be rushed. Establishing boundaries or blocking feelings may come naturally but softening to vulnerability can lead to greater emotional intimacy. They also benefit from shifting away from rumination over rewards or obsession with accomplishments. Spirituality and meditation are self-soothing practices that help them feel balanced.

Venus in Capricorn

Associated with Saturnian energy, Venus in Capricorn can be parental in their relationships, meeting everyone's needs. This can lend a sternness or nurturing role to them. Venus in Capricorn can be a lover of luxury, and giving and receiving physical gifts can be a deeply meaningful expression of love to them. Since Venus in Capricorn can be both mature and caretaking, acts of service for others is a way they express compassion. Accomplishments, pay raises, and promotions can be closely tied to their sense of self-value, and they must be careful not to cross the line into losing their self-worth to external validation or their professional success.

They benefit from avoiding inner stubbornness, power struggles, and controlling relationship dynamics—which they can encounter more than most. Even intimacy can be tied to themes of dominance and control for Venus in Capricorn.

Venus in Capricorn can feel deeply connected to their possessions and gravitate toward elevated aesthetics. A tailored wardrobe, flawless accessories, and meticulous home décor are trademarks of their style.

The Partner for Capricorn Sun and Venus

Despite a sometimes stern, all-business exterior, you long for a partner who makes you melt. Emotional awareness and sensitivity are incredibly attractive to you. An all-in partner who values commitment will be vital for establishing the safety you desire and allowing you to concentrate on building your empire. A partner who brings out your silly side can be a keeper. As the sign associated with the house of the public eye and reputation, you crave a partner who can share an occasional spotlight with you and won't shy away from the camera if the moment requires it. You need a partner who is confident *and* recognizes your self-assurance. You benefit from financially savvy partners in tune with the value of their work. Being respected for your abilities will be important, but you don't crave redundant flattery or fawning. A suitable partner will support your ambition and show patience when you spend long nights at the office or devote yourself to the grind.

With all that intense work energy, there's a mask that can come off in your partnerships or during a night out with friends. If it's not a perpetual coping mechanism, unwinding from pressure through going out usually serves you well.

Shadow Work for Capricorn
The Shadow Traits: Obsession, Control
The Evolved Traits: Surrender, Balance

The Lesson
Ruled by Saturn and opposite the rulership of the moon, Capricorn is on the axis of parental energies. The life lesson for Capricorn is in learning to nurture yourself. Specifically, this will be done through paternal instincts, such as incorporating discipline into routine and embracing rest when necessary. The lesson revolves around cultivating these abilities for yourself and not over-prioritizing everyone's needs.

The Advice
You tend to act out in seasons of change or when not in control. Sometimes, you hide or support your vices via an enabling environment. But the truth is that you're too good for those habits. You're highly capable, but focusing on achievement can teeter into obsession. Relinquish the reins so you don't funnel your energy into unhealthy endeavors.

The Shadow Through Tarot
In the reverse, the themes of addiction, obsession, or toxicity are emphasized in the Devil card. The couple is still chained, and their entrapment becomes highlighted, signifying that a toxic dynamic is blocking your connection to yourself and your self-sufficiency. Maybe you've prioritized someone's opinion at the expense of your values. This card in reverse can also mean that materialism has taken over. A relinquishing of materialism and focus on spirituality are needed. You can benefit from reconnecting with your intuitive nature.

Reflections for Capricorn

+ How can I more intentionally tap into my intuition?
+ Where is my energy distribution out of balance?
+ Where might it benefit me to be in receptive energy and rely on my faith in the Divine?
+ How can I create a greater work/life balance?

Affirmations for Capricorn

+ When my heart and mind are working in harmony, I achieve what is in my highest good.
+ I recognize the value that my expertise and structure bring to projects.
+ Beyond my achievements or the recognition of others, I am worthy of love.
+ My external work is not a measure of my personal value.

Practices for Capricorn Energy

Bring It Back to Your "Why"

In your climb to the top, it's easy to lose sight of your personal reasons for the trek. Realigning with your values and adjusting accordingly is a life lesson for you. And knowing to surrender the goal when it's no longer in alignment indicates evolution. Resist the urge to steadily climb uphill just because you can.

Connect with Your Intuition

As a cardinal earth sign, it's easy for you to become too grounded and lose touch with the precious parts of you. Reconnecting with your higher self or the Divine is an intentional practice that will help keep things in perspective. Nurture your spiritual practice and watch your life bloom.

Practice Intentional Self-Care

Capricorn is the sign associated with reputation and achievement, and a lot could hinge on others and their perceptions. Even though you're more than capable of taking care of yourself, it's easy to let good habits fall by the wayside in the race to the top. Make yourself a priority again. Create a sanctuary out of your home. Cook a nourishing meal. Take an Epsom salt bath. Engage in solo activities that feed your spirit by taking good care of your body and mind.

Go Off-Grid

The professional and familial pressures can take their toll, and reconnection with the natural world for a spell can work wonders for you. You do tend to take on the heavier load for the teams you grace, and being inaccessible can be a nervous system reset. Walk through the woods, invest in a national park trip, or knock a tech-free experience off your long-term goal list. Whichever avenue you choose, allow yourself to indulge in the luxury of detachment.

Chapter Fifteen
Aquarius

Theme: The Change Agent
Archetype: The Humanitarian
Dates: January 20–February 18
Motto: "I know."
Ruling Planets: Saturn, Uranus
House: 11th
Degrees: 11, 23
Modality: Fixed
Element: Air
Color: Blue
Body Correlation: Circulatory System, Synaptic Networks
Keywords: Liberating, Aloof, Revolutionary, Visionary, Unconventional
Tarot Card: The Star

Characters and Celebrities with Aquarius Energy

+ Athena
+ Thomas Edison

+ Harriet Tubman
+ Nikola Tesla
+ Oprah
+ Bob Marley

Aquarius Playlist

+ "Rebel Rebel" by David Bowie
+ "I'd Love to Change the World" by Ten Years After
+ "Sign o' the Times" by Prince
+ "Virtual Insanity" by Jamiroquai
+ "Everybody Is a Star" by Sly and the Family Stone
+ "Moonage Daydream" by David Bowie

Herbs and Supplements for Aquarius

+ Skullcap for stress relief
+ Fish oils for cognitive support
+ Spearmint for alertness

Crystals for Aquarius

+ Aquamarine for connecting with the voice
+ Red or yellow jasper for grounding
+ Kunzite for heart healing and compassion

In a Quote

"I don't really want to become normal, average, standard. I want merely to gain in strength, in the courage to live out my life more fully.... I want to develop even more original and more unconventional traits."

—**Anaïs Nin**

To understand fixed air, we need to understand their natural habitat. Imagine you're inside of a balloon. You're capable of soaring high, but it's not too comfortable, right? Eventually, you're soaring solo and feeling claustrophobic. It is imperative for Aquarius to create environments that suit their nature, but it benefits them to avoid rigidity. Part of the lesson for Aquarius is navigating pivots in life, which usually involves enacting change sooner than they would like. Motivated by progressive change, Aquarius is moving the collective needle toward new, revolutionized ways of being. Effortlessly, they hold a higher standard and unique perspective. When it comes to humanitarian ideals, they have the capacity to be quite selfless. But as a performer willing to dance to the beat of their own drum, they are often ten steps ahead of us. Does the unconventional benefit from involvement in more practical matters? And do we get the opportunity to be changed for the sake of these Aquarian ideals? If the answer is yes, then change becomes manifest here on earth. If not, the Aquarius takes off searching for a new planet of their choosing—one that exists in greater harmony—and they aren't looking back.

In the Tarot

Aquarius's symbol is the water bearer, and because of the symbolism, Aquarius is an air sign often mistaken for a water sign. While water isn't Aquarius's element, their collective empathy is recognized and is represented in their tarot card. The tarot card for Aquarius is the Star card. On it, we find the nurturing water bearer. While depicted in nature, she is more akin to a celestial being. Of all the major arcana cards connected

to the signs, this mystical, star-studded illustration can impart a cosmic feeling. Like the archangel on Sagittarius's Temperance card, the water bearer balances her weight between the water and the earth. Overhead, the night sky reveals eight prominent stars—one large and seven small—symbolically linked to the chakras. In one hand, the water bearer pours water on the ground, gently carving out tributaries and nourishing the earth. With her other hand, she pours water into a large natural pool. Symbolism is woven throughout this card, the waters and conglomeration of stars pointing toward consciousness awakening. This card embodies our rising from the ashes after the dark night of the soul. It is a card of deep healing. This development is in sync with our progression through the archetypes. Once we reach Aquarius, we discover a newfound sense of healing and gather awareness of the collective. This point in our journey involves contributing to a group larger than our own.

Aquarius Sun

Aquarius suns are natural trailblazers in style and with their ideas. As natural activists, they tend to have big hearts for humanitarian causes and can be inspired to lead movements, regularly raising awareness of human rights issues. They tend to follow technological trends and, no matter their age, remain informed of high-tech developments. They also tend to be very engaged on social media. Despite their practical involvement and inspired connection to humanity, they follow their own path and can find vulnerability challenging. Not easily swayed, they can be rigid in pursuing what they believe to be right. This echoes the Aquarian motto, "I know." This knowingness is doggedly determined; at times, they'll need to gently deprogram themselves from what they've committed to as fact. Their high vantage point can make them seem aloof in their relationships. They need open-minded communities, quirky friends, and liberating environments.

Aquarius Rising

Observers of the world, Aquarius risings are motivated by their desire to understand. With a fearless and initiative-taking nature, Aquarius risings tend to stand out in crowds. While they might withdraw their wisdom from the world, they are unafraid of the spotlight. But their sense of self-worth is not tied to the attention of or accolades from others. Like Venus in Aquarius, they can have an eclectic wardrobe, including an affinity for sparkly metallics.

Aquarius rising is future focused, and their ideas can meet resistance simply because their audience, large or small, isn't ready to receive their insights. They illuminate through offering solutions to world issues and progressive ideas. Rejection of their ideas can result in a resistance to share, but they are not quick to change their minds unless motivated from within themselves. They reserve their vulnerable side and most outlandish ideas for their romantic partners and family members with whom they feel the most kinship.

Aquarius Moon

Aquarius moons tend to overanalyze emotions, and they can seem emotionally detached. They deal very well with high-stress scenarios requiring a calm presence. Aquarius moons can feel like they must navigate the world alone and habitually go within or seek solitude. This can leave them feeling misunderstood. It can be challenging for them to be vulnerable, but they benefit from greater transparency and expression.

A collector of knowledge, they are interesting conversationalists. They may surprise you with expertise on topics like outer space and conspiracy theories. A naturally creative placement, Aquarius moons might transmute their feelings into works of art. Processing feelings through regular creativity helps them transmute energy and benefits their well-being. Their self-expression may take an unconventional or dramatic flair, and they may gravitate toward the performing arts.

Aquarius moons carry a sense of responsibility for their lives, contributing meaningfully to society. They want to know they fought for causes they believed in and used time and resources like the precious commodities they are.

Venus in Aquarius

Venus in Aquarius can come off as cold, detached, or simply too cool. This can attract partners with anxious attachment styles, determined to break through Aquarius's cool exterior, as though affection were a prize to be won. Venus in Aquarius can be distracted by their own pursuits, and they may need to be impressed by your wit to invest in you. But just like befriending a cat, you will need to attract Aquarius's attention or accept that it's not for you.

Their style is often unconventional, blending many patterns or colors. Typically, they are unafraid of bright colors and clashing prints in their wardrobe and are comfortable standing out for their colorful, thoughtful outfit. Despite the Aquarian association with the future, they can have a strong affinity for bygone eras, and this presents itself in their clothing choices and home décor. But, at some point in life, something futuristic involving space or aliens typically finds its way into their aesthetic.

In matters of the heart, they can be attracted to mysterious qualities in their partners. Their mental dexterity is up for the challenge of getting to know a more secretive or multifaceted partner. They appreciate partners who give them the room to roam—both physically and mentally. Usually, this freedom gives Aquarius the space for their creative projects, which can be avant-garde and forward thinking. Partners who can appreciate their creations while allowing Aquarius space to produce them are keepers.

The Partner for Aquarius Sun and Venus

Although you don't seek out the spotlight, you appreciate confidence and self-reliance in a partner. Charisma and radiance are vital components to your lasting bond—along with someone who lets you dance to the beat of your own drum. Senses of humor and originality in your partners warm your heart and match your idiosyncratic love language, a symbiosis of quirk and intelligence.

In business and love, Aquarius doesn't take well to controlling or parental types of partners. They don't need to lead the group or be the central focus, but they have too much of an egalitarian and independent streak to surrender to bossiness in others. Aquarius devotes significant energy and time to projects and creative work, making them natural entrepreneurs. They enjoy learning the various roles that entrepreneurship often requires. Aquarius's partner benefits from either being part of these projects or contributing to richly meaningful work that requires a commitment of their time and energy. Either way, Aquarius's partner will need to be understanding of their devotion to their creations.

Shadow Work for Aquarius

The Shadow Traits: Rigidity, Detachment
The Evolved Traits: Progression, Connection

The Lesson

The lesson for Aquarius revolves around their motto, "I know." They are accumulating wisdom and meant to guide others, which generally comes easily for them. But on their unique path, they can feel isolated. The lesson for Aquarius is to be open to the possibility that there is *more* to learn and that this might be found through vulnerability within their community. Finding suitable, nurturing, and stimulating environments is the prescription.

The Advice

With the motto "I know," you can live in your mind and share valuable insights. But you need to allow the evolution of your mindset and not cloak your vantage point from others. You don't have to hold the thought so rigidly. Speak and express yourself. When presented with new facts, will you be willing to shift?

The Shadow Through Tarot

The Star card in the reverse indicates a lack of healing. The spiritual imagery throughout can make us feel spiritually disconnected and longing for a remembrance of our connection to the Divine and a grander plan. This card in reverse indicates the need to connect with water and your intuition and seek healing methods.

Reflections for Aquarius

- What commitments could benefit from the intentional investing of my energy?
- What dream or fantasy can I start bringing into tangible reality?

+ How can I utilize the gifts I've learned from my healing and offer them to others?
+ When can I carve out the space for a mindfulness practice in my routine?

Affirmations for Aquarius

+ I accept that I may have to lead the pack; not everyone will be on board or ready.
+ I understand my commitment to service is not a measure of my value.
+ My wisdom is valuable.
+ It is safe for me to share, and the perfect time is now.

Practices for Aquarius Energy

Practice Vulnerability

As fixed air, you are seen as aloof—even when you deeply care! This can require you to infuse more intentionality into your relationships. Learn the love languages of those closest to you and let them know you care. And while you're letting a real or perceived guard down, allow yourself to receive from others.

Share Your Wisdom

As the wise elder of the air sign trio, you have a message combined with a vantage point that can help others. Put your faith and emotion into action. You have a heart for service, and if it has been a while since you've gotten involved in a cause dear to your heart, answer the call and find an organization or group that could use your help.

Infuse Your Life with Your Creativity and Values

This comes naturally to you. But tying together your creative expression, community, and values aligns you with your natural gifts. Get your friends involved in the projects, activities, or causes that excite you, and stay connected to your creative passions.

Honor Your Eccentricity

With Pluto exalted in your sign and Uranus as a ruling planet, you aren't meant to blend into the crowd. Whether it's through dress, mannerisms, or beliefs, the way you move in the world is going to be distinctive—and might be unpredictable to others. Allow your eccentric side to show and your unique flair to be honored through your everyday life.

Chapter Sixteen
Pisces

Ⅹ

Theme: The Bigger Picture
Archetype: The Healer
Dates: February 19–March 20
Motto: "I believe."
Ruling Planets: Neptune, Jupiter
House: 12th
Degrees: 12, 24
Modality: Mutable
Element: Water
Color: Light Green
Body Correlation: Lymphatic System, Pineal and Pituitary Glands,
    Feet
Keywords: Empathetic, Psychic, Escapist, Selfless, Romantic
Tarot Card: The Moon

Characters and Celebrities with Pisces Energy

+ Pythia, the high priestess and oracle of Delphi
+ The Martyr Archetype
+ A Dream Interpreter
+ The Reformed Addict, like Jim Carroll
+ Jesus
+ Anthony William, the Medical Medium
+ Caroline Myss

Pisces Playlist

+ "The Healer" by Erykah Badu
+ "See You Again" by Tyler the Creator with Kali Uchis
+ "Cosmic Dancer" by T. Rex
+ "Ocean" by The Velvet Underground
+ "The House of the Rising Sun" by The Animals
+ "Angel" by Gavin Friday

Herbs and Supplements for Pisces

+ Blue lotus for intuitive support
+ Mugwort for energetic clearing
+ Calendula for energy regulation

Crystals for Pisces

+ Chrysocolla for emotional expression
+ Lapis lazuli for supporting intuitive connection
+ Black obsidian for grounding and protection

In a Quote

"Although I am a typical loner in daily life, my consciousness of belonging to the invisible community of those who strive for truth, beauty, and justice has preserved me from feeling isolated."

—Albert Einstein

Mutable water is that mist that floats off the surface of a wave and rests on your skin. It's like a generous gift from nature that you didn't expect and can't see, leaving you with a feeling instead of a tangible takeaway. This is the realm that Pisces dwells in. It makes you question reality and wonder what could exist beyond our current level of consciousness. This energy challenges our preconceived beliefs around the deepest topics. It flips them all on their heads for the sake of detaching or perspective rather than judgment. It lives for the dream and the potential gifts awaiting us when we surrender. For Pisces, the dreamscape feels like home. But is leaving the dream or escaping into the dream intentional? Is there purposeful avoidance of life via the dream? And if nothing is actualized from imaginings, are they just ephemera? The answers could all be yes or no, and Pisces might find the questions irrelevant, asking in return, "Does the answer really matter?"

Pisces is symbolized by two fish. This wistful image of two fish swirling around each other feels pacifying, even if we can't pinpoint why. This undefinable sphere is the realm of Piscean energy. Again, does the reason matter if a peaceful feeling is attained? On the healing axis opposite of Virgo, Pisces is a sign of self-sacrifice, higher consciousness, and spiritual connection.

In the Tarot

The card for Pisces is the Moon. On it, we find a dog and a wolf under the moon, and a pathway stretches from the horizon to the water's edge, where a lobster emerges. In this depiction, the three creatures gaze or gesture toward the moon, representing the Piscean twelfth-house theme of the subconscious. As the mysterious scene suggests, this is a card associated with secrets and the unknown, and it beckons us to probe our answers. Intuition plays an integral part. When we

pull the Moon card, there is often a subconscious element that would offer us the answers we're seeking. Generally, there's a piece of the puzzle missing, and the full picture is not clear. This suggests answers lurking within the shadow and invites us for a meditative inner journey to arrive at a conclusion. The Piscean themes of surrender and spirituality are strong.

Pisces Sun

Pisces suns are highly intuitive and can be natural spiritual teachers or wellness professionals, guiding others to discover more about themselves and elevate into their next chapters. They are highly creative and admire the creative gifts in others. They usually have a passionate love for music and dance, accompanied by an extensive music collection.

Neptune, one of their ruling planets, either encourages illusion or dissolves boundaries, and they naturally see past boundaries, propaganda, and constructs that restrict us. As a result, they are prone to seeing things others haven't discovered yet.

Out of fear of being misunderstood, they can be mysterious with their knowledge. Associated with the twelfth house of seclusion, they can feel cast out by certain groups or self-isolate to process challenges. They won't always feel understood, but sharing their knowledge or needs can help them feel connected. They usually enjoy meditation and benefit from spiritual practices to connect with their higher selves or the Divine. Often, when they don't have healthy routines or don't feel connected to their intuition, they can lean toward addictive substances. Pisces sun, rising, or moon should be more wary of this avoidance through dependence than other signs.

A sign of service, they empathize heavily with the cares of their loved ones and the concerns of the world. Pisces sun and rising tend to identify as clairsentient, or having a deep sense of knowing without evidence. Sometimes, that boundaryless Neptunian fog can cloud their vision, and they must have healthy boundaries. In their service, they must avoid martyrdom.

Pisces Rising

Pisces rising is here to understand the world through spirituality, dream states, and healing practices. They interact and communicate in tender, romantic ways; some are natural poets. Breaking out of the box others try to fit them into, they can spend their lives resisting the status quo and are often misunderstood. Without bypassing dreams, they need to be wary of overprioritizing the fantasy realm. The trick may be to continue fantasizing but keep the dream rooted in reality via practical steps.

Like Pisces suns, they can be creative, insightful, and adaptable. They can feel continually drawn to bodies of water, and this may become connected to their spiritual practice. They interact with life as though everything is art, can become musicians or painters, and are whimsical in how they dress and accessorize. They commonly wear accessories tied to nature, incorporating crystals, moon shapes, or natural feathers that carry a deeper significance. In their wardrobe, they favor soft and neutral tones over bright and bold statement pieces. When they are ungrounded, they can appear to be scattered and prone to talk about broad concepts, spirituality, or fantasy. They are not strangers to conspiracy theories and can be curious about plant medicines. They must be careful around fixation or addiction—even to the healthy things.

Pisces Moon

As a psychic placement, Pisces moons might be captivated by past lives, the astral realm, or dream interpretation. They are natural empaths who tend to feel the weight of the world and should be wary of empathizing to the detriment of their well-being. Their sensitivity may cause them to shut down and isolate when overwhelmed. They must implement healthy boundaries for nourishing and recharging. During rocky seasons, they need to prioritize their joy more than most signs. Despite isolation being an easy default, they should express their feelings and allow themselves to feel seen by friends, family, and partners. Understanding past lives and ancestral knowledge can soothe their worry and help them make sense of life.

Despite a structured routine being beneficial for Pisces moons, a lack of structure in their creative life also benefits them. They excel in work projects that provide some guidelines with ample wiggle room to create without feeling confined. They are highly romantic, and their previous partners may become muses in their creative works.

Venus in Pisces

With a yearning for deep intimacy and dreamy romance, Venus in Pisces is a lover to their core. Unfortunately, their tendency to withdraw can lead to struggles expressing their affections. The feelings are there, but there's a wall between their genuine feelings and their expression of them, and that can feel like a perilous wall to scale. Even when they come off as detached or far away, they are available, usually forgiving, and deeply invested. They can be attracted to people who are projects or in deep healing. The martyr theme associated with their energy often manifests as unconditional love in their relationships. Fantastical in love, they can be swept up in a vision of someone, and they benefit from clarity in who they are and around their own desires—even if that clarity is just for themselves. Intimacy for them is heart connected and can be a spiritual act.

Their style can be difficult to define. Their wardrobe tends to be flowy and creative. While their feelings are tied to their aesthetic, they aren't driven by the desire to impress. They want to feel good, and their dress or accessories can take on different meanings or become costumes. Their accessories and home décor hold great spiritual significance and can include crystals, feathers, or anything to clear energy within their space.

The Partner for Pisces Sun and Venus

Their ideal mate is the perfect combination of grounded and psychic. They crave a strong spiritual connection with their partner, and for their well-being, they need the space to forget about *doing* and just *be*. A partner who lets them dream and go down creative rabbit holes but provides them with a sense of security will likely win their heart.

In long-term relationships, clear communication and consistency from partners complement their fluid nature. They benefit from partners who are practical and grounded, possibly handling the minutiae of daily life, like managing budgets. Emotional availability is a must for Pisces's partner.

Because of their fluidity, Pisces can easily find themselves in long-term relationships with close friends. As a water sign, they like establishing trust and the safety of being vulnerable before continuing to share themselves. In business and love partnerships, they must be aware that their lack of boundaries can allow too many opinions into their affairs with others. They will need to practice discernment around topics that involve their partnerships more than most.

Shadow Work for Pisces

The Shadow Traits: Avoidance, Hopelessness
The Evolved Traits: Enlightenment, Perspective

The Lesson

The creativity and selflessness of Piscean energy is a gift to the world. But detachment from the world or neglect of their needs leaves them feeling unfulfilled. They can be prone to intermittent periods marked by a lack of motivation or lethargy. Without neglecting their natural gifts and fluidity, Pisces must tap into their drive and take practical steps toward their dreams.

The Advice

You don't have to go it alone. You feel profoundly and sense the unspoken cues in your environment. But this doesn't mean you are destined to live a life of solitude or in energetic overload. Your loved ones value you and probably want to support you more than you recognize. Create your close inner circle. Express your needs. Without sequestering yourself, take breaks when you need to, and regularly remind yourself that you've got this.

The Shadow Through Tarot

The Moon in the reverse points toward disillusionment or deception. This can emphasize the message of the card in the upright position, which indicates that a current situation lacks clarity and answers have yet to surface. In the reverse, the message is taken even further, and confusion or fear may be present. Opening to truth and seeking guidance will present solutions. The need for going within is highlighted, and connecting with intuition or dreams can provide wisdom for moving forward.

Reflections for Pisces

+ How can I incorporate my intuition into my career?
+ Do I allow myself enough quiet time to recharge and fill my cup?
+ Am I wearing rose-colored glasses or experiencing haziness in my relationships? How can I eliminate that fog or haziness?
+ What practices exist for my mental escape? And how do I manage my time spent in those?

Affirmations for Pisces

+ I know that my superpower is my intuition, and I trust in my inner knowing.
+ When I trust myself to be vulnerable and share, the rewards are expansive for myself and others.
+ I do not have to sacrifice to be found worthy.
+ My dreams are worth being alchemized into tangible creative form and being shared.

Practices for Pisces Energy

Communicate Your Needs

Service comes naturally, and this can easily produce one-sided dynamics. Speak up for your heart, and seek clarity through wellness practitioners, such as healers and therapists, when you feel unsupported. People in your inner circle want to give, but they might not know how to serve you. Tell those you love what you need and open yourself up to receive.

Clear Your Energy

Energy hygiene matters for your well-being. Instead of ruminating or escaping through a not-so-great habit, incorporate energy-clearing rituals into your routine. Put your feet on the grass and ground in nature. Recharge by meditating near a large body of water. Use your deep feelings as an inspiration to create. Then, lean into your community and social circles.

Tend to the Mundane

With Neptune as your ruling planet, staying in a dreamy haze comes naturally for you and lends to your creative work. Sometimes, practical matters fall by the wayside during your biggest creative breakthroughs. You may need to get your ducks in a row more intentionally. Incorporate rituals into routines that feed your practical nourishment, such as cooking, eating well, and tending to your physical health.

Nurture Your Senses

With Venus exalted in your sign, intentionally connecting with your senses will benefit you. This will calm your nerves and guide you toward a grounded state for satisfaction in the present moment. Explore different ways to engage with your senses. For a place to start, indulge in a cozy bedtime tea, determine your ideal scent for daily wear, or register for a sound bath.

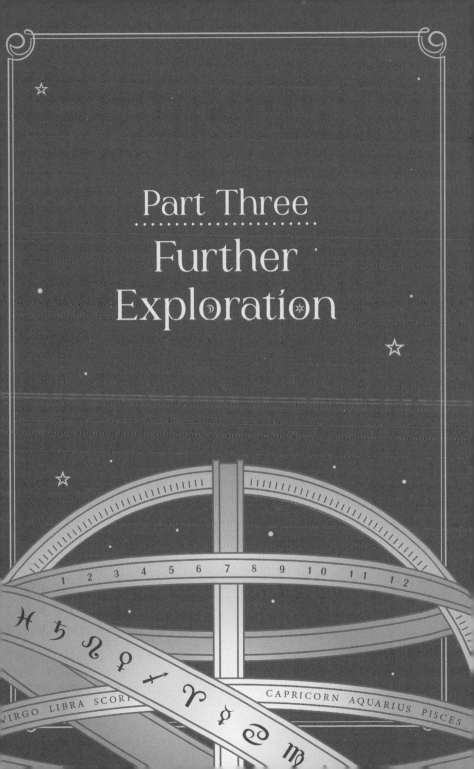

Part Three

Further Exploration

Chapter Seventeen
Intuitive Gifts
· ·

On the path of intentional inner work, as we embark on a process of soul reconnection, we can discover that we are intuitive, spiritually connected beings—and this means that there is a piece of us tied into something greater than ourselves. We might develop a connection to our intuition, and those who identify as sensitive or intuitive beings can find this self-recognition in their charts in multiple ways. Now that you understand the houses, signs, and planets, you might have an inkling about which placements might be more spiritual.

This chapter is meant to equip you with this knowledge so you can apply it to your chart and feel recognized for who you really are. These ten specific placements can identify a deeper connection with this greater universal knowing and your ability to be more sensitively tapped into your intuition. These can also be viewed as highly spiritual placements. Since these are found in various ways, these chart signatures are meant to provide some clarity or assurance, but this is not an all-inclusive list. If you don't have these specific placements, this doesn't negate your intuitive abilities or spiritual connection. Also, when these transits aspect our natal charts, these specific times can indicate more spiritual periods for us or jump-start the path toward deeper connection with our intuitive guidance.

These placements tend to have a more permeable energetic field. They might more easily feel the energy that others are going through and merge this, consciously or not, with their energy. Just as they pick up on the energy of others, they might tend to hold this in their energetic field or body. The need for energetic awareness, protection, and clearing is more relevant for these placements. You might turn to methods for clearing your aura, such as reconnecting with nature or healing with energy work to stay aligned with yourself and feeling well. While we've covered these astrological points referenced, we'll demystify the north and south nodes in chapter 21.

Sun, Moon, or Your Ruling Planet in the Twelfth House

There's a deep connectivity here with the twelfth house themes of the astral realm, dream states, and spiritual guidance (whether termed angels, guides, ancestors, or something else). For sun in the twelfth, you're perceived as having a spiritual nature or wisdom. Sun-in-the-twelfth natives benefit from solitary time to recharge and may need to exert more energy to feel seen in the world. If your ruling planet is in the twelfth, you may need to work with this energy intentionally. For example, if Mercury is your ruling planet in the twelfth, you'll need to intentionally share your voice and not avoid communication. If your moon is here, you'll need to intentionally dig into your feelings. The need to communicate your emotions is a life theme, too.

Mercury in the Eighth or Twelfth House

For either of these placements, you can be curious to understand spiritual lineages, mystical practices, and divination tools. You may feel deeply fulfilled teaching or sharing this material, and your awareness may be more intuitive than learned. In the eighth house, this can be more connected to tarot, astrology, or numerology. In the twelfth house, this can be tied to ancestral connection, energy healing, or dream interpretation.

Uranus Conjunct South Node or the Descendant

Both placements bring deep spiritual awareness and creative connection. Your creativity can involve intense, quick revelations, and projects may be executed quickly. You can shake up the status quo and bring unique insight to societal norms. You may have awareness of past life trauma around being the black sheep or society's outcast. This can be seen as a gift but also a hurdle to overcome.

Mercury in Gemini or Virgo

Mercury in either sign of rulership can indicate important intuitive messages. Holding on to these, writing them, or speaking them will be up to you. But these can be impactful, and you may feel intuitively guided to share.

Moon in Cancer, Scorpio, or Pisces

The moon in water signs can be soft and sensitive to picking up on the energies of others. At times, it might be challenging to determine what is your baggage and what is your loved one's concerns that you are energetically carrying. You benefit from energetic clearing practices, such as smoke cleansing and salt baths, to keep your auric or energetic field clear.

Stellium in Sixth, Eighth, or Twelfth Houses

Healing work can be indicated with these specific stelliums, and your intuition can be your inner rudder as you navigate daily life. When clear, healthy, and feeling well, others may sense your healing energy. Your routine will be most significant if the stellium is found in your sixth house, your interpersonal relationships are the target if it's in your eighth house, and your inner spiritual world is the focus with a twelfth-house stellium.

Neptune Conjunct the Sun, Moon, or Mercury or in the Fourth, Eighth, or Twelfth Houses

Mythologically tied to the oceans, Neptune embodies a mystical, dreamy, and untamed quality that mimics creative inspiration. Also, as a planet of spirituality, Neptune conjunct the sun, moon, or Mercury lends spiritual themes to your sense of self, intuition, or communication. Likely, any one of these placements would impact your perception of your surroundings and ability to detect unspoken cues. Your dreams could feel significant and offer premonitions. The need to routinely perform grounding exercises or be in nature could be significant. Likewise, Neptune in these three houses denotes a rich inner life where spirituality and your intuition could play a significant role throughout your life. In the fourth house, there can be a connection between your sense of spiritual connectivity and your ancestry. In the eighth and twelfth houses, you might feel spiritually connected and enriched through your creative practices.

North Node in Gemini, Virgo, Scorpio, or Pisces or the Third, Sixth, Eighth, or Twelfth Houses

In addition to being an intuitive placement, your intuition may play a part in your life's work or your purpose. As you lean into spiritual practices that feel aligned with you and pique your curiosity, you'll feel a greater sense of inner fulfillment. Healing practices, being of service professionally, or providing healing messages for others could be significant throughout life.

South Node in Virgo, Scorpio, Pisces, or the Third, Sixth, Eighth, or Twelfth Houses

As the placement indicating your deep knowing, these south nodes found in these particular signs and houses signify energies of healing and intuition that are understood on an intrinsic level. These also reveal past lives where healing, guiding, and communication could have been significant. We can utilize the lessons from these experiences again in this lifetime.

Chiron Conjunct North Node, South Node, Ascendant, or Descendant (Especially in the Sixth, Eighth, or Twelfth Houses or in Virgo, Scorpio, or Pisces)

With this placement, purpose is combined with the healing of self and offering it to others. With Virgo or the sixth, this could be in practical or medicinal ways. For Scorpio or the eighth house, this could involve uncovering hidden information, perhaps through astrology or tarot, that can help others heal themselves or gain knowledge. For Pisces or the twelfth, this could manifest as a spiritual leader, energy healer, or guide through addiction recovery.

Big Gifts in a Tiny Nutshell

In our modern world, it is easy to disconnect from our gifts and strengths and to live unaligned with our purpose. Understanding the placements tied into our spiritual nature can help us better understand ourselves on a soul level. Through our interpretation of these placements, we move past the superficial.

Chapter Eighteen
Jupiter's Blessings

The largest planet in our solar system, Jupiter is the planet of blessings, and generosity and limitlessness are tied to Jupiterian ways. Mythologically, Jupiter, or Zeus, is tied to the symbolism of the lightning bolt, majestic eagle, and sturdy oak tree. Whether Roman or Greek, there is a strength embodied through this energy that presided over the skies. This strength can be indicated through our Jupiter placement.

Jupiter in our natal charts reveals an area of our lives in which we can receive gifts and experience ease throughout life, and the sign and house provide us with custom cues. This energy is known to expand, which can be for our benefit or detriment. Opportunity is tied to this expansiveness, and we can find some nods toward its shadow and take note for awareness.

In the following sections, we'll explore Jupiter's role through each of the signs and twelve houses. For clarity on Jupiter in your chart, explore the sections for the sign and house of your personal placement. These will guide you toward seeing how you can find greater ease and experience potential blessings. This is where opportunities can blossom. Also, look to any aspects between Jupiter and other planets or

198 • Chapter Eighteen

luminaries in your chart. This will relay how the energy of abundance and expansion communicates with another placement. For example, if you have Venus conjunct Jupiter, this reveals tendencies to overindulge and an affinity for the finer things in life, and it can reveal romance as highly prized. Looking to the themes of this house can offer more clues, and in this example, this will be tied to higher spending in this compartment of life. Also, the sign associated with your Jupiter placement lends clues to long-term partnership—traits you're likely to embrace and your partner can embody.

Jupiter in Aries and the First House

You can have an incredible, healthy relationship with yourself and your physical body. You may have great clarity around who you are and security in your personality. Your presence can be magnanimous and draw others to you, and you can have a tremendous impact on your immediate environment. There can be a magnetism surrounding you, but be cautious. In its shadow, this could manifest as bossiness or someone viewed as dominating in their environment. In the first house, this can manifest as having presence and experiencing opportunities when you embark on a solo project or launch. Your individual experiences may bring you great benefit. Your natural strengths can be taking initiative, being a boss, and embarking on self-reliant work.

Jupiter in Taurus or the Second House

This is a positive placement for self-esteem as well as your relationship with resources. You might find that you build personal wealth or earn money easily. While you're supported in managing personal finances, Jupiter doesn't do all the heavy lifting. You can benefit the most from this placement by meeting it halfway. This includes managing your assets, budgeting, and being in healthy environments for your self-esteem. Focus on sensual pleasures, financial stability, and self-worth, as these are your natural strengths.

Jupiter in Gemini or the Third House

This is a beneficial placement for networking, communicating, and building community. Keen to exchange information and ideas, this placement implies a curious lens on life and a hunger for knowledge. Your knowledge is more than book knowledge; it is found through learning, conversation, or firsthand experience. At various points in life, this can indicate blessings through your local community and pleasant relationships with siblings and neighbors. The shadow to sidestep is not becoming so comfortable in your local surroundings that you avoid traveling and venturing into the unknown. Your natural strengths are having a unique perspective, offering data, and exploring new interests.

Jupiter in Cancer or the Fourth House

With this placement, feeling lucky comes from your family and private life. You are skilled at creating cozy environments and driven to cultivate a peaceful home life. It's likely that being with close family is where you feel most empowered and fulfilled, and you can find comfort through hospitality and cooking. But this placement's shadow is the temptation to ignore new connections and avoid taking risks when connecting with those outside your immediate circle. Don't overlook your life and relationships outside of your family. Tapping into your nurturing energy can be beneficial for you, as well as focusing on intuitive development. Cultivating a fulfilling private life, finding comfort at home, and caring for family are your natural gifts.

Jupiter in Leo or the Fifth House

You can feel easily connected to your creative gifts and authentic expression. You likely have a magnetic quality or feel like you're meant to be *center stage* in some area of your life. Courageously expressing yourself aligns you with your true nature. Fulfilling the desires of your inner child is healing for you. The shadow of this placement rears its head when you seek approval from an audience. Self-gratification and assurance will be key for inner balance. Creativity, self-expression, and connecting with children (or being childlike) are your natural gifts.

Jupiter in Virgo or the Sixth House

There is abundance found in sticking with a routine, and this might come naturally to you. This can be a very fortunate placement for health and well-being, and you might find you have lots of energy. The shadow for this placement is found in taking health for granted. Jupiter's energy likes to meet us halfway, and giving intentional effort to your physical well-being will take you far. Whether giving or receiving, you benefit deeply from healing practices, such as bodywork or energy work, or any practice that improves well-being. This placement indicates ease with organizing your space and tasks, and it can indicate ease in your leadership endeavors or work collaborations. Meticulous execution in your work, healing abilities, and a mystical connectivity to nature are your natural gifts.

Jupiter in Libra or the Seventh House

For this placement, blessings can be found through relationships, marriage, or business partnerships. Court cases can resolve in your favor and offer beneficial outcomes, and there can be fortuitous results in situations with others, restoring balance and harmony. A strong connection can be formed to art, music, and themes of harmony, justice, and peace. While you have a gift for seeing many perspectives, the shadow of this placement is indecisiveness. As someone capable of emotionally detaching to grasp the larger picture, knowing which principles are worth fighting for is paramount. Your natural gifts include harmonious partnerships, artistic capabilities, and a natural sense of diplomacy.

Jupiter in Scorpio or the Eighth House

Helping others to heal themselves and the ability to learn hidden esoteric knowledge are connected to this placement. Embracing transformation, overcoming adversity, and understanding psychology might come easily for you. As the sign and house of obsession, you must avoid rumination to combat the shadow side of this placement. Blessings through partnerships, high-grossing collaborations, or financial gifts bestowed through others can be relevant. Favorable business deals or marriage, spiritual gifts, and understanding mysteries of the Universe are your natural gifts.

Jupiter in Sagittarius or the Ninth House

Absorbing knowledge and becoming a teacher, especially of religion, of spirituality, or in higher learning, are likely with this placement. You can discover great teachers in life and stumble upon gurus that shape your path. Your faith and beliefs will be important drivers for future decisions. Be careful that your beliefs don't become concrete dogmas, incapable of shifting when presented with new information. You may uncover blessings through travel, especially in places where you don't speak the native language. Adventures can connect you with the essence of yourself, and you might identify as an explorer or world traveler. Having encyclopedic knowledge, learning through adventures, and offering higher perspectives can be your natural gifts.

Jupiter in Capricorn or the Tenth House

Focusing on achievement can be effortless for you and may lead directly into management positions and CEO status. You may experience ease with developing systems and leading groups and complex organizations, and your reputation can be repeatedly blessed throughout life. There can also be blessings tied to your legacy. Staying on the straight and narrow and devoting energy to your work could be all the heavy lifting that this placement requires for success. But avoid achievement at the cost of sacrificing everything else. If you're not mindful, your relationships can take the back seat, and other priorities can get neglected at the cost of success. Leadership abilities, administrative skills, and setting standards for productivity are your natural gifts.

Jupiter in Aquarius or the Eleventh House

Having original ideas and expressing yourself in a unique way are common for this placement. Your avant-garde thinking can stimulate new possibilities for others or initiate new movements. Involvement in humanitarian causes and being of service are likely priorities that bring rewards. Avoid frustration when others don't grasp or see your vision, and understand that your ideas could form a chasm between you and others. But building community and a vast network can come easily. Your natural gifts are offering your unique outlook, openness to radical change, and having your finger on a futuristic pulse.

Jupiter in Pisces or the Twelfth House

Living in alignment with your intuitive knowledge can come easily for this placement. You might identify as psychic or have any of the *clair* senses, such as clairvoyance. You might be highly talented in dance or musical fields and have a vivid imagination. You may find abundance through time spent in solitude, and your creative and meditative life can be important parts of these blessings. This placement is also tied to spiritual protection, and this can be encapsulated in the common phrase "rejection is protection." Recharging through solitary time or spiritual practices is important and advised. Be careful that solitude doesn't become isolation, as this can be a natural reflex. Heartfelt servitude can come naturally, but it can shift into martyrdom. Be sure to prioritize your personal needs. Extrasensory awareness, blossoming creativity, and serving others are your natural gifts.

Chapter Nineteen
The Wounded Healer—
Chiron and Our Well-Being

Our knowledge of astrology expands as new celestial bodies are identified this happened when Chiron was discovered. Chiron is an asteroid that drifts between Saturn and Uranus, a link formed between the Saturnian theme of restriction and Uranus's desire to break free. While Chiron takes fifty years to orbit the sun, its elliptical orbit means that its time in each sign varies, spending about seven years in some signs and just one or two years in others.

In mythology, Chiron was half man and half horse, favored by Apollo, and a well-studied healer of many curative modalities. Chiron was immortal yet injured by Hercules's arrow, and as his "wounded healer" title suggests, he was capable of healing others but incapable of self-healing.

Our Chiron placement can reveal deep-seated wounds, and these are tied into our childhoods. Like in the myth, this is where we need healing and where we empathize and help others but find it challenging to help ourselves. This reveals where we can feel inadequate and need greater gentleness with ourselves and an area in need of attention. This placement can also signal wounding we may have encountered in past lives.

Facing and healing the wounds associated with our Chiron placement can be intentional and intense work. To release the energy of trauma that has been stored in the body, we can engage in healing methods that honor the natural connectivity between our mind, body, and spirit. It may involve therapy, astrology, bodywork, or energy healing to remove residual energy and address blocks.

This is where we can become a voice for the voiceless and those who share the same struggle. The combination of house placement and sign will reveal the most information.

Chiron and Virgo Energy

Chiron was discovered in 1977 by Charles Kowal. In 1987, an astrologer named Barbara Hand Clow made a case for Chiron being the ruling planet of Virgo. This offers depth and insight into understanding Virgo and, perhaps, complements our awareness of Chiron, too. Sharing a service-focused axis with Pisces, Virgo is undoubtedly a healing sign and energy. Considering Virgo's restorative gifts and their sense that they can't meet the standard they set for themselves, the lens of healing is a helpful one. It lends grace and compassion to Virgo energies and a call for their own self-compassion.

Chiron in the First House or in Aries

Associated with personal themes, this placement reveals a wound in our relationship with ourselves. Early in life, your sense of self-worth was probably impacted. Insecurity around identity can result in repeated quests to discover yourself or susceptibility to manipulation as others project onto you who they may want you to be. This placement can also indicate insecurity in your relationship with your physical body. It's important to build self-empowerment in healthy and proactive ways. Cultivating a loving relationship with your physical body is important and can entail a conscious investment of your energy. Honor yourself and your unique journey through life. Self-honesty will be healing for you and align you with supportive relationships.

Chiron in the Second House or in Taurus

This placement is tied to wounding around finances and resources. Early in life, a lack of resources could have left feelings of scarcity and financial insecurity. Like the first house, this house also indicates wounding around self-worth or perception of your value. Feeding a healthy sense of self and fostering abundance in mind, energy, and resource management are healing focal points. Heal money blocks and explore positive mindset work through affirmations or another practice. Avoid hoarding or stagnancy in your relationship with money, and explore calculated risk. Accepting that your self-worth is not tied to any harmful early life messages will be crucial.

Chiron in the Third House or in Gemini

This placement reflects wounds around communication and connection. You might have difficulty getting your point across, feeling as though your message lands on deaf ears. In some cases, past-life wounding from speaking your truth could manifest as a speech impediment. There could be residual childhood wounds stemming from your local community or elementary school years. This might manifest through multiple moves or feeling like you didn't belong. This can also indicate wounds in your relationships with siblings. No matter how it is received, you are worthy of sharing your story and truth. You must accept that your voice matters—and lends a necessary and unique perspective. Allow your curiosity to guide the way, knowing that you are a connector of perspectives with the capacity to be a channel. You might also heal others or find healing through your voice, possibly by singing, or with your hands.

Chiron in the Fourth House or in Cancer

This placement carries wounding around a sense of family and home. You may have incurred trauma in your teenage years and carry wounds specific to a mother or a caretaking figure. You may long for a sense of home and feel like you are on a lifelong quest to find belonging, comfort, and security. You may benefit from therapy around family trauma and building a found family instead of forcing bonds with your birth family. Honor your emotional needs and sensitivity and form connections with emotionally available people. Healing your ancestral line, learning about your ancestors, and nurturing yourself can be deeply healing.

Chiron in the Fifth House or in Leo

For this placement, there can be wounding related to your sense of expression or creativity. You could feel guilt or shame for sharing joy. When you were growing up, your creative gifts or personal expression could have been mocked, and you might feel insecure about being the main character in your life. Tapping into your childlike side or embracing a sense of wonder could feel uncomfortable. You will need to be intentional in seeking joy and pleasure. Embracing your happiness is critical and will naturally heal childhood wounds. You must heal your relationship with creativity and discover your worthiness to be center stage. Allow your light to shine and take emboldened action toward your heart's desires. You can and should be the main character in your life.

Chiron in the Sixth House or in Virgo

With this placement, you might identify as a perfectionist or worrier. In childhood, you could've been placed in anxiety-inducing scenarios or faced the threat of worst-case scenarios, which could've led to nervousness or digestive issues. You heal from intentionally calming your nervous system, calming your mind, and rewiring neural pathways with new stories surrounding your safety and peace. Breath work, yoga, and performing mindfulness exercises could be helpful regular practices for you. Also, building a schedule that supports your growth is a helpful focal point. Accept that you are safe and well despite ingrained fears. Supportive health routines, daily rituals, and acts of service are healing for you. Accept that you are not perfect—and that is more than okay.

Chiron in the Seventh House or in Libra

For this placement, wounding shows up through partnerships. In childhood, you may have witnessed difficult partnerships or the breaking of bonds, leaving a confusing blueprint for healthy relationships. You may have lacked examples of reciprocal or balanced relationships. In adulthood, there could be a misconception around energy exchange in partnerships, and either overgiving or withholding could be manifestations of these early lessons. This early information could spill into business affairs or marital matters. Intentionally seeking information or counseling around relationships, learning healthy give-and-take, and healing old relationship wounds can be life-changing.

Chiron in the Eighth House or in Scorpio

For this placement in a house of energy exchanges, there could be wounding around intimacy, vulnerability, or trusting others. There could've been early childhood events that raised deep existential questions about life's fragility and the afterlife. You may have felt a pressure to grow up fast. As a result, you might feel like pieces of your innocence or childhood are missing. Reclaiming childlike joy and simultaneously healing traumas through therapy is medicinal for you. Also, exercising discernment in contracts without blocking out new partnerships will be critical. You can facilitate healing others' wounds and heal around topics others find challenging.

Chiron in the Ninth House or in Sagittarius

For this placement, childhood wounding could be related to a religious organization, spiritual group, or authority figure. There could have been a teacher, professor, or guru-type figure that left some scars. For healing, indoctrination might need to be explored as well as healing feelings of shame for divergent thinking, especially if you felt cast out for your beliefs. You might not feel ready to teach or lead others despite being the right fit for an influential position. Not waiting for some so-called *perfect* moment and accepting your knowledge and skills are healing. Accepting that you're worthy of leading others, developing a relationship with your intuition, and trusting new teachers can be the medicine.

Chiron in the Tenth House or in Capricorn

For this placement, there could be early trauma connected to institutions or corporations. There might be wounding around public recognition or how the public perceives you. Like Chiron in Cancer, there could be a strained and stressful family connection and trauma related to a paternal figure or your father's side. Learning to nurture yourself and heal your inner child will be key. Trusting that you can be a leader and successful in your career is also important. Despite any past pains in the spotlight, you can heal reputation-related wounds and begin anew. Embrace your honest childhood experience and reject any belief to maintain the status quo that relies on suppressing your truth.

Chiron in the Eleventh House or in Aquarius

This placement can experience childhood wounding around friendships or social networks. There could've been wounding experienced from long-distance travel or moves. You could have perpetually felt like an outsider, and your deepest desire can be to belong. Building healing friendships in adulthood will be necessary. Intentionally developing new connections and nurturing the bonds can be healing. Any inner child healing work around moving or travel should be addressed, possibly through therapy. For this placement, being true to yourself, particularly your uniqueness and eccentricity, will be important. As you continue connecting to your truth and value, the right community should embrace you and recognize your value, too.

Chiron in the Twelfth House or in Pisces

For this placement, your spiritual beliefs could have left you feeling outcast or like you didn't belong. You may identify as having any of the extrasensory perceptions, such as being claircognizant or clairvoyant. These abilities could've left you feeling misunderstood in childhood, and at some point, you felt pressure to blend in and suppress your sense of natural wonder. You benefit from accepting your intuitive gifts and cultivating a lifestyle that supports your intuition and spirituality. You need supportive, nonjudgmental friendships where you feel accepted for your gifts and who you are. Your wounding might be hidden from the world, and it benefits you to confide your hidden fears to someone you love or an intuitive healer. Seeking energy healing, shamanic healers, and spiritual readers can provide wisdom and strength. You might also heal well privately—as long as your healing work is intentional.

Chapter Twenty
Pluto—The Route to Empowerment

Pluto is an indomitable force. It destroys and transforms. Furthest from the sun, the purposeful wrecking ball travels a long, winding road, and this slow approach ensures long-lasting change. Pluto's journey reflects what we know about transformation—change takes time. Pluto and pivotal moments ask us to go deeper. In terms of personal development, the journey to greater assurance requires honest assessment and a stripping of the superficial. The mile markers along our Pluto journey are memorable, activating moments that teach us our power, which often happen through feeling like we don't have it. As much as Plutonian energy involves and allows decay, it is also concerned with harnessing the ability to regenerate anew.

Our Pluto placement is not our inherently understood power position. In fact, it's commonly a superpower others witness and is not self-detected well. It is a position of *potential* strength. That ability for others to witness this strength can draw opportunistic or parasitic energy into our lives, leaving us feeling disempowered. But that

214 · Chapter Twenty

214 · Chapter Twenty

aftermath isn't reflective of our genuine fortitude. Harnessing the potency of our Pluto placement requires self-recognition.

Power and Control

Until we recognize these inner assets, we run the risk of control battles in this area of life. For example, if you have Pluto in your fifth house of dating and creativity, you could enter partnerships with people who compete with you, and your partner's admirers may be in silent competition with you. It will be advised to release controlling tendencies within and be wary of them from partners. Also, by sharing your creative musings and recognizing you're in competition with no one, you step more fully into this Pluto-in-the-fifth-house placement.

As a celebrity example, Britney Spears has Pluto in her first house of self and body. By developing a strong, healthy connection to herself, specifically her physical body, she is able to powerfully perform and attract attention. This empowerment has enabled her to secure a lucrative career. However, control over her personal expression has been a life theme and has been tied to manipulation in relationships and domination within family. By reclaiming her personal responsibility with the willingness to cut ties with oppressive individuals, she asserts her power position and takes an impactful leading role in her life. Wherever Pluto lies in our natal chart, we are called to maintain a healthy sense of responsibility and assurance—and it can reflect where we must stand up for ourselves.

Pluto Through the Houses

The house and sign of our Pluto placement offer clues about where we can be an inimitable force. But secrets, trauma, and psychological components can all be themes for your exploration surrounding your Pluto placement. So, it can be valuable to examine this position through two lenses. The first involves exploring how trauma relating to the themes of your Pluto house and sign has weaved its way into your understanding of life. Investigate how these impacts may have shifted your awareness of yourself and reflect on themes of control here. The second lens involves embracing this energy as your personal superpower. You have innate gifts in this part of your life. If you've been denying these abilities, now is a good time to clean the residue from these past wounds and connect with these powerful pieces of your wiring.

Pluto in the First House or Aries

Embrace: Self-Empowerment
Avoid: Codependency

This placement suggests power in taking the individual route. You can feel evoked to take new uncharted paths and seek out the unfamiliar. Whether you acknowledge it or not, you can be a born leader. It's important for you to lean into self-sufficiency, as life events can arise that reveal codependency as poison. Power struggles may be initiated by others. Tending to your physical health and body can be a source of strength and empowerment. While self-discipline may be a strong suit, be wary of dogged self-restriction through rigid routines. Your self-sufficiency can be judged as intimidating, but your initiative and drive are superpowers.

Deep Dive Exercise

Journal about three ways that exhibiting self-control has benefited you and your physical health. For deeper inquiry, reflect on how you have stood up for yourself in your relationships and how prioritizing your personal needs has led to rewards.

Pluto in the Second House or Taurus

Embrace: Resource Management
Avoid: Frivolous Spending

This placement holds potential power in your sense of self-value and command over finances. There can be strong determination around managing resources and acquiring affluence. Others can notice this determination. Throughout life, there can be the potential for transformation regarding one's personal resources. At times, you may experience self-worth challenges, which can be due to unfair treatment from others. You may feel the need to be defensive or protective in relationships, but the lessons revolve around recognizing your personal strength and ability to source confidence from within. Acknowledging and healing these traits can bring about a remarkable resilience and a healthy awareness of your self-value. You can be presented with life lessons where you must discern when it's best to stand resolute or to surrender to change.

Deep Dive Exercise

Name three or more practices that have helped you consciously manage your resources. If this exercise presents challenges, investigate a tool or app that could assist with managing time, money, or assets.

Pluto in the Third House or Gemini

Embrace: Connection
Avoid: Suppression

This position carries tremendous persuasive power and a gifted ability to communicate. You could thrive in sales and hold a powerful position within your local community. Transformational opportunities can arise within your neighborhood or city, and as life unfolds, you may redefine what community means to you. Your relationship with siblings could be significant, and you may be a source of strength in these relationships. The weight of your words and witnessing their impact could be a lifelong exploration. You'll benefit from exploring the topic of control and your voice. Explore instances where silence was used to control (whether that was self-motivated or externally expected). Instances of bullying around your truth could be significant to heal. Developing your relationship with your voice and sharing it through writing or broadcasting can be constructive and healing.

Deep Dive Exercise
Draw awareness and hold gratitude for the times you've used your voice to stand your ground, experience deep connection, or impact your community. Journal about some of these instances.

Pluto in the Fourth House or Cancer
Embrace: Personal Power
Avoid: Naivete with Family

This placement reveals a powerful connection to your inner realm, home life, and maternal line. Your ability to navigate challenging family dynamics could be an asset, but this tool may be discovered through trial-by-fire scenarios evoking your inner warrior. Topics to heal could include battling with black-sheep dynamics in the family or controlling dynamics in your upbringing or lineage. This placement can also indicate a powerful capability to break free from these unhealthy bonds. Your superpower can be your sense of connection and ability to provide nurturance.

Deep Dive Exercise

Notice the role you've played in your birth family and found family. Journal on how assertion has benefited you or impacted your close relationships. Reflect on nurturance as a source of strength—both for yourself and loved ones.

Pluto in the Fifth House or Leo

Embrace: Creativity
Avoid: Self-Neglect

Your gifts may lie in your creative capabilities. Your self-expression is unique, and you are not meant to follow trends; it's more likely that you'll set them. Your voice matters, and expression is a virtue. So, be your own muse. In childhood, you could've encountered scenarios of jealousy or feeling like it was more powerful to suppress your needs and passions. Expressing them is not only your superpower but also has the capacity to heal this old wound. You may have experienced controlling tendencies from romantic partners as well. Releasing the grip of past partners through grief and acceptance could be significant for breakthroughs.

Deep Dive Exercise

Reflect on the ways creativity and expression have impacted and shaped your life. For more illumination, journal on your past potent creations and breakthroughs learned from romance.

Pluto in the Sixth House or Virgo

Embrace: Ritual
Avoid: Perfectionism

In this house and sign of healing, you can find strength through solving issues for others' well-being. You have the ability to be a powerful force in the workplace and in day-to-day life. You'll want to be wary of power struggles with coworkers. Your presence could be healing, and you may bring solutions through smart, analytical talents. You are a powerful healer, and your transformative abilities can be tied to health and rituals that benefit others. Don't belittle your gifts just because others have been intimidated by you in the past. Don't shrink because you feel inadequate or imperfect. Claim your wisdom in practical and mystical ways. Your medicine is valuable, but it doesn't define your inherent value.

Deep Dive Exercise

List the ways your routine supports you and the practices that have become a source of empowerment. If you need, schedule three rituals to begin integrating into your week that provide structure and self-soothing.

Pluto in the Seventh House or Libra

Embrace: Diplomacy
Avoid: Control Tactics

This placement is associated with partnerships and indicates that you'll need to discover your sense of self-value within the context of relationships. This will require you to not outsource your power and to recognize how much value you bring to shared dynamics. You've likely had controlling partners or family members, and you'll need to avoid exerting your will and controlling others, too. Part of your life lesson revolves around this surrender of controlling partnerships. You'll also want to avoid placating or people-pleasing to hold relationships together. Your superpower lies in diplomacy and emotional connectivity while avoiding codependency.

Deep Dive Exercise

Take a moment to reflect on past hardships in your relationships. Try to identify the emotions that arise as they relate to grief and notice where you can soften into forgiveness or acceptance of past situations. Consider doing a meditation around forgiveness. If you find you need to clear the air, consider doing so or writing a letter you can decide to dispose of, send, or keep to yourself.

Pluto in the Eighth House or Scorpio

Embrace: Sharing
Avoid: Obsession

This placement has a strong ability to handle the undertow in life. Managing deep or taboo topics that are psychological in nature can be your strong suit. For healing, you'll want to explore themes of security and resources from early years. Your boundaries being crossed may also be a topic to investigate. In your shared contracts or resources, be wary of dominating tendencies in yourself or others. Notice and manage obsessive tendencies, especially around shared resources, romantic partners, or spiritual practices. Your ability to help others heal their repressed stories and traumas can be deeply meaningful. Marital counseling, occult studies, or investigative work could be significant and strong fields of study for you.

Deep Dive Exercise

For the sake of awareness and healing, take a moment to reflect on any repetitive themes from business or romantic partnerships in your past. Journal about these and notice any new insights around these experiences.

Pluto in the Ninth House or Sagittarius
Embrace: Learning Through Experience
Avoid: Inflexibility in Beliefs

Your talents can lie in acquiring knowledge and disseminating it through teaching others. Powerful guides may come into your life, but there could be some encounters with controlling mentors. Healing wounds relating to control from superiors, teachers, or religious figures could be significant. In younger years, a dogmatic vantage point can take hold. Transformative trips or pilgrimages can be significant, and with greater life experience and worldly exploration, you acquire knowledge. This activates your ability to teach from a solid foundation void of rigidity or naivete. Your ability to guide others can be your superpower, and you're likely to lead others from a place of optimism.

Deep Dive Exercise
Explore the influence of teaching and teachers as well as the role travel has played in your life. List the takeaways from any international or long-distance trips, and journal on the knowledge and skill sets you've acquired through your educational and travel experiences.

Pluto in the Tenth House or Capricorn
Embrace: Leadership
Avoid: Rigidity

This placement can feel at home in the public arena and being seen. They will likely be in the public eye and closely identify with their career. Cosmic repercussions could be public, so walking the ethical straight-and-narrow road will be imperative. Regarding your reputation, it may

222 • Chapter Twenty

feel like there's a tightrope on which you must balance. At times, you may need to stand up for yourself, and knowing when to surrender and lose the battle to win the war will be important. Transformation can happen through your career, and you have a strong capacity to leave a legacy. Your impact can reveal itself through political roles as well.

Deep Dive Exercise

Explore the topics of empowerment through career milestones. Journal about the role of relationships in helping or hindering your achievements and deep dive into reflection and gratitude for your successes.

Pluto in the Eleventh House or Aquarius

Embrace: Eccentricity
Avoid: Groupthink

In group dynamics, you are a powerful force. You could have a commanding presence within tech fields or social media. Sharing data and forming community could be easy talents, and you have a strong ability to bring together people with like-minded ideals. This ability can arise through the formation of any group, especially ones related to activism or something futuristic and progressive. While you'll want to avoid using controlling tendencies within group dynamics, you aren't meant to just blend in either. Also, be wary of any group attempting to control you. Expression within the group and sharing ideals can prove significant and healing.

Deep Dive Exercise

Journal about the times you've danced to the beat of your own drum. Take this further by exploring the ripple effects of your self-expression, your impact in communities, and the values that surface from these actions.

Pluto in the Twelfth House or Pisces

Embrace: Spirituality
Avoid: Dependency

This placement suggests potential strengths found through spiritual and healing fields. But monitoring your hidden beliefs is important, as self-doubts or outsourcing your personal power could be potential obstacles. If any self-defeating thoughts creep in, you will benefit from addressing these head-on. It will be essential to embrace divine timing and universal love, and this may come naturally. Surrendering to meditative and dream states might be instinctive, and energy healing may be of interest. Your spiritual practice and targeting your inner world should be a place of refuge and have the potential to shift your outer world for the better. But be wary of control dynamics within any spiritual group. You can be a positive influential force in healing, rehabilitation, or shamanic work in the world.

Deep Dive Exercise

If you haven't already, begin the practice of working with a dream journal. If it resonates, use this for post-meditative work as well, capturing insights from meditative states onto paper.

Chapter Twenty-One
The Nodes—
A Purposeful Life

When looking for deeper purpose in our charts, which may or may not relate to our career, we are looking for our north node placement. The north node carries significant messages related to the lessons we are learning in this lifetime, and it is one of the most important placements for finding fulfillment.

The north and south nodes of the moon are two points that travel along an orbital path, crossing the sun's ecliptic. They are always in opposition to one another, and these move in retrograde. They transit each sign for about eighteen months. Some online charts will only reveal the north node symbol. So while it's not visibly present, your south node is sitting directly across from your north node placement sharing the same degree.

In Indian Vedic astrology, or Jyotish, the nodes are associated with a dragon. Jyotish's ancient roots influenced the tropical Western, or modern, form of astrology taught widely today and in this book. The north node, or Rahu, signifies the head of the dragon and can have an insatiable appetite. Rahu is connected to fate and is mostly beneficial. The warning is that its path can become a point of obsession.

The south node, or Ketu, is the tail of the dragon. Our south node placement reveals the knowledge we have learned from past life-times—it's what we already know and is comfortable. This node can represent a field of study or soul knowing that we likely mastered in a past life. These skills are valuable and should come naturally. But this isn't the path we're meant to maintain. Instead of being complacent in our south node, we are stretched by moving into our north node.

Our north node is our north star. It is a key indicator of our soul's purpose, and moving into alignment with it can feel like a stretch—but for most, it isn't too scary of a hurdle. A push to get us there might come in the form of motivation or education but will likely involve detachment from an easier route into one with greater satisfaction.

Approximately every eighteen and a half years, the nodes return to their placements in our natal charts. When the transiting nodes return to their places in your natal chart, this marks a time when fated events transpire and change is inevitable. You will naturally feel magnetized toward the themes of your specific north node placement, and something associated with the themes of your south node is likely to leave your life. For example, if you have the north node in Capricorn or your tenth house and the south node in Cancer or your fourth house, you may experience an invigorated pull toward your career (a tenth-house theme). You'll have a hunger to excel and might network and take the initiative to grow your position within your field.

The south node in your fourth house can manifest in a few ways. During this career-focused time, you will likely invest less energy into your home and family life. You could naturally reassess your current living situation and move to a new home. If something is plaguing your inner life, you might be letting it go at this time. For example, if you've been shy or self-conscious around socializing, you might over-come the hurdle during this transit and develop an ease with social events and professional mixers. You might release an aspect of your home life and bypass a blockage relating to your inner world as you strive toward newfound achievements. Regardless of your nodal placements, during your nodal return, you can feel pressure to shift or experience changes occurring outside of your control, and this is an opportunity to recalibrate your life in alignment with your honest de-sires. In some areas of life, it is time to blaze a new trail.

The house, sign, and degree of our north and south node place-ments lend more clues about our purpose and soul knowing. Tak-ing all three of these into account provides the fuller meaning of our nodal placements, but a great place to begin is with the north and south node placements through the houses.

North Node in the First House and South Node in the Seventh House

Embrace: Independence
Avoid: Self-Abandoning Relationships

This is the hero's journey. You are learning the value of autonomy and self-sufficiency. Particular times have required you to break free from partnerships and blaze a solo path. Also, there are times in life when you feel urgency to focus on your physical body or health. Your south node indicates an understanding of relationships from a past-life his-tory of partnership. Collaborating and considering others is your nat-ural inclination. But the lesson in this lifetime is to break free from codependent tendencies or enmeshed relationships, learn to feel well in solitude, and make independent decisions.

Deep Dive Prompts
- Where do I allow others to make decisions for me?
- Where (or to whom) do I hand over my autonomy?
- How can I better care for my own needs?

North Node in the Second House and South Node in the Eighth House

Embrace: Self-Value

Avoid: Enmeshment

Like someone who has the south node in the seventh house, you understand how to be a partner and consider others in your decision-making. This awareness can include sharing resources, finances, or collective belongings, which might come naturally. However, in this lifetime, your life lesson centers around the management of your *personal* finances and resources. There are lessons to be learned around self-sufficiency and cultivating self-worth without the foundation of external validation. You might also have an inherent understanding of deep spiritual or occult knowledge. The satisfactory path can be found by bridging the gap between spiritual and practical matters, ultimately incorporating more practicality into life and building a stable foundation.

Deep Dive Prompts
- How can I boost my self-worth in a healthy way?
- Which environments are nourishing and self-worth reflective?
- What's one step I can take toward better managing my resources?

North Node in the Third House and South Node in the Ninth House

Embrace: Inquisitiveness
Avoid: Stubbornness

For this nodal placement, there is comfort in teaching others. There can be a natural inclination to write, teach, or become a community leader. You might have awareness around a specific spiritual practice or religious leadership from your past lives. However, your lesson now is to follow your curiosity and learn new things. Gathering and sharing information is aligned with your satisfaction. Becoming a lifelong student may benefit you. Also, while there might be a continual desire to travel the world, your lesson is cultivating community and investing energy into your local surroundings.

Deep Dive Prompts

+ How can I nourish my curiosity?
+ What has left me feeling inspired lately?
+ Where can I find new information to inspire fresh thoughts?

North Node in the Fourth House and South Node in the Tenth House

Embrace: Family Interconnectivity
Avoid: Overprioritizing Reputation

For this placement, focusing on your career and public life creates a sense of security. You may make decisions based on your reputation or the opinions of others. With this public focus as your default, the value of your inner life could fall by the wayside. In this lifetime, giving attention to family and shifting the emphasis from your public to your private life is critical. Sometimes, you will feel pressured to abandon workaholism or networking to prioritize your immediate family. Whether with birth or found family, focusing on strengthening these familial bonds creates true satisfaction for you.

Deep Dive Prompts
+ What can I do to improve my home life?
+ Which close bonds need nourishing?
+ Do I need to restructure my schedule to prioritize my family or inner life?

North Node in the Fifth House and South Node in the Eleventh House

Embrace: Creative Expression
Avoid: Self-Suppression

You are learning to embrace creativity and be in the spotlight of your life. You are here to embrace main character energy; by contrast, you might gravitate toward humanitarian causes. There can be an inherent focus on serving others and charity, and you could be aware of this altruism from previous lifetimes. You could be best suited for creative work where leadership and heart-centeredness are tied to life's purpose. Your personal expression and inner child healing could play a role in your legacy. Aligning with joy and radiating it to others is an important part of your destiny as well.

Deep Dive Prompts
+ What can I do to align more with ease and joy?
+ How can I cultivate my creative gifts?
+ Am I too comfortable giving, and do I reveal my worthiness to receive?

North Node in the Sixth House and South Node in the Twelfth House

Embrace: Structure, Healing
Avoid: Disorganization, Escapism

With your nodal placements on this axis of healing, you have spiritual gifts from your past, and you might hold remembrance of being a shaman or a healer. However, in this lifetime, you are learning how to take this sense of service and care for yourself and others in practical ways. You might catalyze intuitive dreams or spiritual knowledge and create something tangible for others with it. Your path could benefit by incorporating analysis and pragmatism. Connecting with the earth, such as working with herbs and plants, might hold significance for your fulfillment. You can be learning to give attention to detail, and you might incorporate spirituality in coaching others.

Deep Dive Prompts
+ Where could perfectionism be holding me back?
+ Which spiritual practice do I feel most pulled toward?
+ How can I nourish myself more through my routine?

North Node in the Seventh House and South Node in the First House

Embrace: Emotional Availability
Avoid: Hyper-Independence

You can carry an awareness of how to live autonomously. You might identify as self-sufficient and crave freedom within your partnerships. At times, you'll feel strong pressure to sacrifice for the sake of compromise. Becoming fluent in vulnerability will be important for you. It is worth accessing your comfort in receiving love from others and exploring the balance between giving and receiving. In this lifetime, you are learning to release your grip on self-sufficiency while sharing yourself through partnerships. While this is likely to show up through marriage, this can be a focus in family and business relationships, too.

Deep Dive Prompts

+ How can I lean more on my partner or loved ones?
+ Where can I allow for more give-and-take in relationships?
+ How can I bring these dynamics more into balance?

North Node in the Eighth House and South Node in the Second House

Embrace: Spirituality, Vulnerability
Avoid: Self-Sufficiency, Harsh Boundaries

Likely, managing your resources and belongings comes naturally to you. You may be self-sufficient and secure in handling your personal finances. The lesson is to learn how to balance shared resources, which may involve managing others' resources, too. Themes of reciprocity and energy exchange are crucial and can manifest as finding emotional balance in partnerships. Drifting from personal focus and toward the value of a shared energy results in soul evolution. Also, your curiosity could extend to occult knowledge, or your purpose could align with uncovering hidden secrets, exploring psychological themes, or intimacy. The practical route could be your reflex, but the spiritual one generates greater fulfillment. You benefit from nurturing your mystical life.

Deep Dive Prompts
+ What are my mystical gifts?
+ How can I better nourish these through a spiritual practice or learning?
+ Is there a partner (romantic or platonic) in need of my insight, gifts, or time?

North Node in the Ninth House and South Node in the Third House

Embrace: Adventure, Leadership
Avoid: Flightiness or Irresponsibility

Cultivating community can come naturally for you. You might gravitate toward social activities, meeting new people, and connecting with your neighbors. You're likely a natural communicator and inherently curious. Your lesson is to expand outside your comfort zone and bring that curiosity into the world. You are also meant to move beyond surface-level inquisitiveness and dive deep into a field, or fields, that interests you. This could manifest through long-distance travel and learning about other cultures. You may feel more satisfied moving beyond a student role and into a professorial one. Professionally, when aligned with this north node energy, you can become a teacher or leader guiding others. Your leadership might be spiritual or religious in nature.

Deep Dive Prompts
+ Where can I invest more effort into my learning?
+ What skills and lessons have I developed well?
+ Professionally or not, am I pursuing a calling that involves teaching others and sharing insights?

North Node in the Tenth House and South Node in the Fourth House

Embrace: Long-Term Planning, Networking Opportunities
Avoid: Short-Term Comfort, Isolation

Your comfort zone can be found through focusing on your personal life and immediate family. It comes naturally to invest in your physical home, and creating a living space that is stable and soothing is intrinsic to you. But this north node placement craves more energy devoted toward your career, legacy, and public life. Leaving the comfortable nest of your immediate circle and focusing on relationships created through networking sparks growth. Long-term planning could bring huge gratification. Devoting time toward developing your reputation and professionalism is part of your journey.

Deep Dive Prompts
+ What's one step I can take to invest in my professional life and those relationships?
+ Do large events or networking opportunities give me social anxiety?
+ If so, how can I combat this or ease my way into these connections?

North Node in the Eleventh House and South Node in the Fifth House

Embrace: Originality, Socializing
Avoid: Conformity, Seclusion

You have natural creative gifts and could feel comfortable expressing them. Your self-expression may magnetize attention. However, your true fulfillment is found through investing energy into an external focus, such as building community or raising awareness around humanitarian rights. Purpose is found through causes larger than yourself, and this might manifest through philanthropy, creative fundraising, or becoming a leader for a marginalized group. You benefit from finding likeminded communities while exercising skepticism instead of subscribing to others' beliefs. Finding innovative life solutions that bridge gaps could be tied to your fulfillment. Also, you may be curious about astrology, space, or technology, and these subjects can be tied to your purpose.

Deep Dive Prompts

- ♦ How do I feel most inspired to serve?
- ♦ Am I invested in a community that understands me?
- ♦ What's one step I can take toward a goal aligned with my natural gifts?

North Node in the Twelfth House and South Node in the Sixth House

Embrace: Service, Spirituality
Avoid: Martyrdom, Addictions

This is a very mystical placement, indicating that you were a healer in a past life and are in this one. You might have high personal standards, focus on practical matters, and overprioritize your work or routine. Summoning grace for yourself is soothing medicine. For satisfaction, the focus is on using your gifts and abilities to serve others. This service might be on a large scale or for an ostracized or stigmatized group. Using gifts related to the astral realm, energy work, quantum healing, or psychic abilities can be connected to your purpose. You benefit from seeking spiritual teachers and healers and serving as one at times. Throughout life, there can be recurring lessons around surrender.

Deep Dive Prompts

- ◆ How can I show myself more grace?
- ◆ What unhealthy habit is overdue for releasing?
- ◆ How do I serve others through my current line of work?

Conclusion

From shadow work to intuitive placements to personality quirks, you have an arsenal of self-awareness material—and this should feel good! As you know, this isn't just a tool for excavation's sake or trendy appeal—astrology is a means of empowerment. You could spend years or decades on a detour others steered you toward, but it isn't your genuine footpath. Considering the lasting impacts of societal conditioning and familial indoctrination, chart interpretation is a divine tool for shining a flashlight down the path toward ourselves. Throughout this book, you've likely had *aha* moments that reflected your true self. Ultimately, while your uniqueness is something to celebrate, understanding this language of the cosmos should help you feel that you are not alone in the Universe.

There is a continuous adventure to be found in your chart. You can take many twists and turns, and as life events unfold, you'll discover more pearls of cosmic wisdom. With this solid foundation to build upon, you'll continue learning how each of these integral pieces forms the whole picture. Jump into the degrees and interpret how these energies apply another layer to your learning. Dive deep into the aspects in your chart. Know that challenging aspects (and transits) refine lead into silver. These challenges are not impossible walls to scale. But they are climbs to conquer and can mold us into new, resilient forms.

With a grasp on your natal astrology, another opportunity for learning is through observing transits and their impacts on your natal chart. In astrology, we see windows. Some windows open into new opportunities. This means that the windows aren't always open. On a soul level, you might feel this, too. Or you might notice in your past where opportunities were portals to new paths, and now, the portal is past. Some examples of this are when a romantic relationship dissolves, an artistic residency completes, a college student graduates or, when in search of a new destination, a bold soul relocates. These windows of change are portals reflected to us in the cosmos, too. Whether pertaining to romance, career, spirituality, or self-development, new portals arrive and correlate with the transits. We are never lone wayfarers, and we are gifted with a celestial compass. While we must surrender to some seasons and allow events to unfold, we can move through some of these portals and act with our will.

Just as our sun sign is not a life sentence but something we are continually blossoming into, your entire chart is this way, and a dance is happening between your free will and these predestined points in life. Some of these choices are yours to take or pass up. As the world continues to shift and our lives inevitably unfold, this is a valuable time to seek cosmic guidance and invest in the one person we are responsible for and can control—ourselves.

Recommended Reading

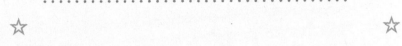

For your next steps on the cosmic journey, here are some astrological resources.

Astrology by Andrea Richards

Chiron: Rainbow Bridge Between the Inner and Outer Planets by Barbara Hand Clow

The Inner Sky: The Dynamic New Astrology for Everyone by Steven Forrest

The Moon Sign Guide: An Astrological Look at Your Inner Life by Annabel Gat

Seventy-Eight Degrees of Wisdom: A Tarot Journey to Self-Awareness (New Edition, 2019) by Rachel Pollack

Signs and Skymates: The Ultimate Guide to Astrological Compatibility by Dossé-Via Trenou

To Write to the Author

If you wish to contact the author or would like more information about this book, please write to the author in care of Llewellyn Worldwide Ltd. and we will forward your request. Both the author and the publisher appreciate hearing from you and learning of your enjoyment of this book and how it has helped you. Llewellyn Worldwide Ltd. cannot guarantee that every letter written to the author can be answered, but all will be forwarded. Please write to:

Catherine Gerdes
℅ Llewellyn Worldwide
2143 Wooddale Drive
Woodbury, MN 55125-2989

Please enclose a self-addressed stamped envelope for reply,
or $1.00 to cover costs. If outside the U.S.A., enclose
an international postal reply coupon.

Many of Llewellyn's authors have websites with additional information and resources. For more information, please visit our website at http://www.llewellyn.com.